NEW ENGLAND SOUP FACTORY
COOKBOOK

By MARJORIE DRUKER
and CLARA SILVERSTEIN

PHOTOGRAPHS *by* RON MANVILLE

HARPER
HORIZON

To Paul and Emily
You stir me with love every day.

Copyright © 2007 by Marjorie Druker and Clara Silverstein

Published by Harper Horizon, an imprint of HarperCollins Focus LLC.

Marjorie Druker: food stylist
Joan Druker: prop stylist
Photography by Ron Manville

Page design by Walter Petrie

ISBN: 978-0-7852-5605-2 (TP)

Library of Congress Cataloging-in-Publication Data

Druker, Marjorie, 1964–
    The New England Soup Factory cookbook / by Marjorie Druker and Clara Silverstein ; photographs by Ron Manville.
        p. cm.
    ISBN-13: 978-1-4016-0300-7
    ISBN-10: 1-4016-0300-9
    1. Soups. 2. New England Soup Factory. I. Silverstein, Clara, 1960– II. Title.
TX757.D78 2007
641.8'13—dc22
                                                                                    2007001361

Table of Contents

Acknowledgments

It took a lot of teamwork to turn the recipes that we make every day at the New England Soup Factory into a finished cookbook. We are grateful to the people who helped us along the way.

We often joked that it is easier to find a husband than a cookbook agent. We found a good professional match in Clare Pelino of Pro Literary Consultants, who believed in our proposal right from the start and successfully took it into the marketplace.

Our publisher and editor, Geoffrey Stone of Rutledge Hill Press, guided us through every step, from finding a consistent format for the recipes to the design for each chapter.

Ron Manville, our photographer, helped capture the food in its most beautiful and vibrant state by working 14 hour days without losing focus, and barely taking a break. Marjorie's mother, Joan Druker, stepped in as prop stylist extraordinaire, finding just the right bowls, spoons, napkins, and flowers for every shot.

Many individuals also deserve personal thanks from each of us:

From Marjorie:

My parents, John and Joan Druker, gave me the ability to understand what I was good at and then lead me there. Starting from when I was young, they exposed me to wonderful and interesting food. It fascinated and thrilled me—and still does.

My sisters, Julie and Janie, are my very best girlfriends in the world, and gave me valuable assistance for this book. I thank Janie for letting me photograph the food in her home, and Julie for helping me to organize and keep the kitchen clean during both photo shoots.

Paul is my other half, my very best friend, and the guiding force in the life of the New England Soup Factory. He has worked hard and never complained. I am most grateful for his contributions, both personally and professionally, in my life.

My daughter, Emily, was the inspiration for me to start a restaurant when she was only three. I knew that when she was born, I needed to work so that I could make sure that she had the opportunities I wanted for her. She supports my efforts, even when she is tired of listening to me. She is truly my mini me.

My beloved grandmothers shared with me great recollections from their pasts so that I could taste the flavors of their lives, and learn about things that only they had seen and experienced. Grandma Florrie was a true foodie who would chat with me for hours about great meals. Grandma Sylvia always made me white linen and lace aprons so that I would look nice when I catered parties.

My mother's best friends always took an interest in my life, and hired me for my first catering jobs. They have also shown me that it is incumbent upon women to develop ourselves both personally and professionally to make the most of our lives and feel accomplished. These amazing women are Sylivia Queen, Beverly Siagel, Vivian Spertner, Renee Zalcman, Elaine Rothstein, Alyce Mandell, and Janie Rodney.

Over the past 12 years, my brothers- and sisters-in-law have always lent us a hand with our business. Whether it was investing in us, or helping us to redesign the store, they were are all there to help. I thank Robby, Alan, Michael, Nancy, Chris, Linda, Andrew, and Jen.

Rosemarie and Tom Brophy, my mother- and father-in-law, have treated me with love and kindness since the day Paul introduced me to them. They raised a son with kindness in his heart, and I am so thankful for how lovely they made him. Their belief in our business made it easier for us to believe in ourselves, and to make our business work.

My devoted and cherished staff shows me their talent and capabilities every day. I admire the quality of their work, and their dedication and loyalty to the New England Soup Factory. Ted, Chris, Steve, Marcello, Daniel, Amy, Roberta, Michael,

Abe, Randy, Leo, Celio, Emilio, and many other employees, both past and present, have contributed to the success of our business.

I thank my friends at the Phantom Gourmet in Boston, Dave, Dan, Eric and Michael, for giving me a platform to show their viewers what we do at New England Soup Factory. Over the past 12 years, they have been more than generous, and I have always enjoyed my experiences on their television show.

Steve Uliss, my friend from high school and college, deserves thanks for inviting me to co-host "All Fired Up!" with him over the past three years. We always have fun while cooking up something delicious.

I knew Clara was special from the day that we met over coffee and tea, and kept talking for something like four hours! I think we both knew that we were a good fit for each other to produce this cookbook. It has been an easy experience to work together and I really admire who she is and what she stands for.

My deepest and most heartfelt thank you goes to every one of my customers. Day in and day out, they eat my soup and tell me how much they love it. They have sought comfort in my food. When I see their faces lined up at the door; it warms my heart. They always enlighten me and give me a sense of purpose. Enjoy this book, and you may discover more inside than just recipes. Dig in!

From Clara:

I have greatly appreciated the chance to work with Marjorie, whose enthusiasm for cooking and willingness to keep experimenting with new recipes, always impresses me. While writing the book, we often joked that two heads are better than one, but I think it's true for this project.

For wise counsel and professional support tempered with a sense of humor, I could always count on the Ladies Who Lunch: Ali Berlow, Carolyn Faye Fox, Andrea Pyenson, Lisë Stern, Rachel Travers, Cathy Walthers, and Lisa Zwirn.

My husband, George, and children, Jordan and Martha, helped me keep everything in perspective. They gave me many great reasons to stop obsessing about exactly the right description for a particular soup, and to just make dinner!

Introduction

My earliest soup memory took place in kindergarten when we were reading Stone Soup. This is a tale about a hungry traveler who comes to a village and announces that he can make soup from a stone. He puts a stone in a pot of water and then asks the villagers to bring ingredients to help the soup along. One person brings an onion, another a carrot, and so on until the soup is made. After we read the story, we made stone soup in class. Each of us brought an ingredient. My mother sent me with Goodman's vegetable soup mix: A cylinder of lentils, green split peas, barley, alphabet noodles, and a seasoning packet. This went into the big pot for our class soup.

At the end of the day, when the teacher gave each of us a Styrofoam cup of soup to take home, I could hardly contain myself. "I really liked the soup!" I blurted out to my teacher. She told me that the special packet of mix that I brought was just perfect because the lentils added flavor and texture. That may have been the beginning of my career, but neither one of us knew it.

In the months and years that followed I discovered that I loved food, and I loved to cook even more. Helping with family meal preparation was not a chore, but a delight. I made a salad each night, standing on a kitchen chair just to reach the counter. I chopped up so many ingredients that it took an hour to make. Cucumbers, carrots, radishes,

Marjorie Druker

sweet red peppers, cherry tomatoes, black olives, and croutons—I threw them all in. My sister, Janie, had to bribe me to leave out the chickpeas. When she offered me a dollar, I tried to negotiate. "Will you give me two dollars if I leave out the olives, too?" I asked. It was a deal.

I still adored soup, too. My mother continued buying the Goodman mixes, but she would always embellish them with other ingredients. She made a large pot every Sunday morning, and by the time we came home from religious school, it was soup time. I could have sat at the kitchen table all day. I was relieved when I started wearing contact lenses because my glasses no longer fogged up while I leaned over a steaming bowl.

When I was in high school, a boy from my youth group called me for a date. He told me that we were going to do something fun, but that it was a surprise. When Saturday came, he picked me up and assured my parents that he would have me home by 10:00 p.m. Then he drove me to his home and gave me a tour, which ended in his family's kitchen. Here was the surprise: He was going to make chicken soup for me. There was already a tall can of broth on the counter, and he took the onions, carrots, celery, and parsley out of the refrigerator. He must have known that he could win my affection with homemade soup.

After working for a gourmet shop in high school, I realized that I wanted to make a career out of cooking. My next destination was culinary school at Johnson & Wales University in Rhode Island. As I was learning to be a professional chef, I met a fellow student who changed my life. In the fall of 1983, when I was nineteen years old, I went to the South Seas Plantation resort on Captiva Island, Florida, for an internship. I arrived at the school during a pouring rainstorm, so exhausted and disoriented that I ended up eating pickle spears and Milano cookies for dinner. The next afternoon, as I talked to my father on the phone in the employee housing dorm, I saw someone down the hall knocking on my door. It turned out to be Paul, the other Johnson & Wales student from Massachusetts. Our school had told us to meet each other. Little did they know we would end up getting married! We ate dinner together that night, and have been together ever since.

At first, Paul and I kept things quiet because we both had to work in the resort's kitchen, but then someone saw Paul whipping eggs for my Hollandaise sauce, which was a dead giveaway! Since then, we have worked with each other on jobs large and small. He has even been a waiter at some of my catering jobs. We both love food and searching for great ingredients. He is the kind of person that you could give a million things to do, and he would handle each task in order and never lose his cool. In the early 1990s, I established a private cooking and catering business, which gave me a flexible schedule so I could spend time with our daughter, who was born in 1992.

The idea of a soup business gradually took shape, as I realized that soup provided the medium I wanted for inventive flavors and combinations. My niche is taking what people like to eat and turning it into a soup. I opened the first New England Soup Factory in 1995 in the Boston suburb of Brookline, Massachusetts. Paul, who has a degree in food service management, has been my partner and worked in the business since the beginning. Three years later, we opened a second location in nearby Newton. All along, we have tried to remain true to our vision of a store specializing in a rotating, seasonal selection of gourmet soups, plus accompaniments—sandwiches, salads, and cookies and dessert bars.

Over the years, we have served thousands of customers and been recognized nationally in *Restaurants & Institutions* magazine, *Nation's Restaurant News, Restaurant & Business* magazine, and *Newsweek*. We have received four "Best of Boston" awards from Boston magazine. I have demonstrated my soups on the Food Network, as well as Boston-area shows including *The Phantom Gourmet*.

I can't claim that every day goes smoothly, or that the stress of owning a business never overwhelms me, but I have never lost my passion for inventing new soup recipes or ladling out our long-term favorites. This collection of recipes gives me a chance to share some of the best recipes that I have developed over the years. They have all been tested on the customers, so I know they are successful. You don't have to put a stone in the pot to experience the pleasure of making your own soup at home. Enjoy these recipes, and, as our store motto goes, Feed Your Body Well.

Equipment and Technique

I'm a chef who likes to cook at home as much as I like to work in a commercial kitchen. I have designed most of these recipes for you to make at home, without special training or equipment. You'll also find most of the ingredients at an ordinary grocery store. I want you to spend most of your time cooking and eating, not running around looking for a particular kind of oil or spice.

Here are just a few notes that will help you follow my recipes more easily:

1) **Stockpot**—I use a heavy 2 to 2 1/2-gallon stockpot with a tight-fitting lid. All-Clad and Calphalon both make high-quality, sturdy pots. Avoid an inexpensive pot made from thin material. It is not likely to conduct heat well, and you will end up burning your ingredients.

2) **Sautéing**—When sautéing vegetables in olive oil, I heat the pot first, then add the olive oil and vegetables. The preheated pot lets the vegetables start to "sweat" (give up their liquid) right away, and to create a flavorful base for the soup. This technique does not work for butter, which burns.

3) **Pureeing**—Many of my soups need to be pureed to thicken the texture and blend the ingredients. I couldn't live without my hand blender (also called an immersion beater). This handheld blender goes right into a pot of soup and purees the contents. A regular blender that sits on the countertop works, too, but it is more cumbersome to use. You have to transfer the hot soup into the blender, usually working in batches because the blender won't hold it all. As you puree, do not place the lid on the blender tightly, as the pressure of the hot liquid can build up and cause an explosion! Put it on loosely and hold your hand over the top to keep it from flying off.

4) **Serving size**—I generally figure on 12 ounces (1 1/2 cups) of soup per person. Even at home, with my family of three, I like to make batches of soup that serve at least 6 people. We can make another meal of the soup or freeze the leftovers. Having a homemade soup on hand is like money in the bank.

5) **Stove temperature**—I have specified high, medium, and low levels of heat on the stove, but every appliance is different. Adjust your burner levels accordingly. Generally, you want to let soup simmer gently, not boil rapidly over high heat.

6) **Vegetarian**—To help you identify vegetarian recipes, I've marked each one with a ⓥ. Many others that are not marked can be adapted by replacing chicken stock with vegetable stock.

Taking Stock

Inseparable from every good soup is a good stock. In this age of hurry-up cooking, it may seem like too much bother to make your own, but your own stock gives your soup a head start on flavor. It adds body and a complex, savory element before you even put the first ingredient into the pot. My stock recipes are simple enough to make in an afternoon. You don't need to fuss over dicing the vegetables into perfect-looking cubes, as they will be strained out. Once the pot is simmering on the stove, you can walk away and do something else for awhile.

Once the stock is strained, let it cool for two hours at room temperature and then refrigerate. As you transfer the stock from the pot, measure it out by the cupful, and label the container so you will know exactly how much you have on hand for any soup. These stocks should all keep for up to three days in the refrigerator.

To freeze a stock, refrigerate it first, then place it in a freezer-safe container. Resealable plastic bags are handy for storing stocks, as they take up less room than traditional plastic containers.

If you are really pressed for time, stock from a can or box will get you through the recipe, but the flavor will be compromised a bit.

When I was eighteen years old, I took a job in the kitchen of Camp Tevya, the summer camp in New Hampshire that I had attended. I already knew that I wanted to go to culinary school, and I needed to help pay for the tuition. Being a third cook was not nearly as fun as being a camper. We fed 450 people three meals a day, plus snacks. Seven days a week, we worked from 5:00 a.m. until 7:30 p.m. I got a two-hour break after we cleaned up from lunch. It was just enough time for a small nap before I had to go back and set up for dinner.

This was without a doubt one of the most grueling jobs that I had ever taken. I was the only female in the kitchen, and the chefs either yelled at me or made fun of me. Each morning I had to go into the slop house to bring out the discarded food for the local farmers to feed their animals. I burned my hands on the Fryolater and had six blisters with bubbles. Once, I even cut myself and needed to get stitches. Whenever I called home, I complained nonstop to my dad. Through it all, he steadfastly refused to let me come home. "Johnson & Wales does not accept quitters into their school," he said.

Since Tevya is a Jewish camp, the biggest and most important meal of the entire week was the Shabbat on Friday evening. We always served chicken soup, and it was my job to prep all of the vegetables. I would start by peeling a fifty-pound bag of onions, then fifty pounds of carrots, which turned my hands bright orange. Then I would wash and trim a whole case of celery. The final step was placing two huge cases of chicken wings into an eighty-gallon kettle, adding the vegetables, and letting it simmer all day. The smell of chicken soup wafted throughout the camp as anticipation built for this important—and popular—meal.

When I look back on this part of my life, I realize that it gave me the right foundation, not only for making gigantic batches of chicken soup, but for succeeding in my chosen profession. I am now grateful that my father made me stay. Just because a job seems too difficult doesn't mean we should walk away and not challenge ourselves. It is through hard work and determination that we learn how to best cope with situations that are not easy, and to keep moving towards our goals.

Clear and Rich Chicken Stock

If you only make one stock from scratch, it should be chicken. For chicken soups, of course, it is absolutely essential. It also seems to miraculously absorb whatever flavors are in the pot, so it can be used in place of beef or fish stock.

6 pounds chicken backs, wings, and/or thighs	1/2 bunch fresh parsley
3 large Spanish onions, peeled and cut into quarters	2 bay leaves
6 ribs celery, cut into thirds	4 chicken bouillon cubes
6 carrots, peeled and cut into thirds	16 cups water, plus more as needed
	Kosher salt, to taste

In a large stockpot place the chicken, onions, celery, carrots, parsley, bay leaves, bouillon, water, and salt. Bring to a boil over medium-high heat. Skim and discard the foam that rises to the top of the pot. Reduce the heat to medium and simmer gently for 3 hours, adding 1 to 2 cups of water if the stock reduces too much. Strain through a colander and discard the solids. Let cool and refrigerate up to 4 days. When the stock is cold, skim off and discard the fat from the top.

Makes 12 cups

Chicken stock becomes even more useful when you freeze it in ice cube trays. When you're making a dish that needs last-minute enrichment, add one of the frozen cubes. It will melt right in and fortify the dish with more intensity and depth. This works really well for gravies, stews, meats, and even marinara sauce. For a shortcut, commercially prepared chicken broth may be used in place of chicken stock.

Fragrant Fish Stock

This stock comes together in about an hour. If you let it simmer too long, it can get bitter. Fish bones can be requested from a fishmonger. Ask for mild flavored fish such as haddock or cod; salmon might add too strong a flavor.

6	pounds fish bones or shrimp shells	1	bunch fresh parsley
2	large onions, peeled and cut into quarters	1 1/2	tablespoons whole peppercorns
6	ribs celery, cut into thirds	2	cups Chablis
4	parsnips, peeled and cut into large pieces	1/2	fresh lemon
4	whole cloves garlic, peeled	8	cups water
2	bay leaves		Kosher salt, to taste

■ In a stockpot, add the fish bones, onions, celery, parsnips, garlic, bay leaves, parsley, peppercorns, Chablis, lemon, water, and salt. Bring to a boil over high heat. Reduce the heat to medium high and simmer for 35 to 40 minutes. Carefully strain the stock through a fine mesh colander or a regular colander lined with cheesecloth. Let cool and refrigerate up to 3 days before using.

Makes 8 cups

Canned clam juice makes a quick substitute for fish stock.

Lobster Stock

Lobster stock is one of my favorite ingredients because it's so potent and adds the distinct flavor of lobster to seafood soups. Once you boil the lobsters and separate the meat from the shells, the stock comes together easily. For once, you don't have to discard the shells.

3   lobsters (1 1/2 pounds each)
1   large Spanish onion, peeled and cut into quarters
3   ribs celery, cut into thirds
3   carrots, peeled and cut into thirds
1 1/2 cups dry white wine or vermouth

1   can (6 ounces) tomato paste
6   to 8 sprigs fresh parsley
    Kosher salt, to taste
3   bay leaves
8   to 10 whole peppercorns
    Water, as needed

▨ Fill an 8 to 10-quart pot with water. Bring to a boil over high heat. Drop the lobsters into the pot. Boil for 8 to 10 minutes. Remove from the pot and let cool until they can be handled. Remove the meat from the shells and refrigerate the meat until ready to use. Reserve the lobster shells and bodies.

▨ In a stockpot place the lobster shells, onion, celery, carrots, wine, tomato paste, parsley, salt, bay leaves, and peppercorns.

Add enough water to cover the lobster shells by 3 inches. Bring to a boil over high heat. Reduce the heat to medium high and simmer 1 1/4 hours, adding 1 to 2 cups of water if the stock reduces too much. Strain through a fine mesh strainer or sieve or a regular colander lined with cheesecloth. Discard the solids. Let cool and refrigerate up to 3 days before using.

Makes 10 cups

This is the only recipe I can think of that places more importance on the lobster shells than on the meat inside. You can feast right away on the lobster meat, and then make the stock, or refrigerate the meat for later use in a salad or a soup recipe, such as Pumpkin, Lobster, and Ginger Soup (see page 136).

Meaty Beef Stock

Beef stock is one of more complicated, time-consuming stocks to prepare, but it yields a tremendous return. It starts with beef bones that are oven-roasted with vegetables to bring out their flavor. The stock also has lots of body, making it a perfect base for beef stew, onion soup, and gravy. It's a perfect project for a snowy day, when you can't leave the house anyway.

6 to 7 pounds beef bones or knuckles	1 tablespoon whole peppercorns
2 large onions, peeled and cut into quarters	2 bay leaves
6 carrots, peeled and cut into thirds	4 beef bouillon cubes
4 ribs celery, cut into thirds	1/4 bunch fresh parsley
1 can (6 ounces) tomato paste	16 cups water, plus more as needed
5 whole cloves garlic, peeled	Kosher salt, to taste

■ Preheat the oven to 450 degrees. In a 13 x 9-inch roasting pan place the beef bones, onions, carrots, and celery. Using a pastry brush, brush the tomato paste over the bones and vegetables. Bake for 40 minutes, or until the bones and vegetables turn brown and a bit caramelized.

■ Transfer the contents of the roasting pan into a stockpot. Add the garlic, peppercorns, bay leaves, bouillon, parsley, water, and salt. Bring to a boil over high heat. Reduce the heat to medium and simmer for 4 hours, adding 1 to 2 cups of water if the stock reduces too much. Strain through a colander and discard the solids. Let cool and refrigerate up to 3 days before using. When the stock is cold, skim off and discard the fat from the top.

Makes 12 cups

Ask for bones from a butcher or from the meat department at a supermarket. You can also use leftovers from a standing rib roast. Store the bones you plan to use in the freezer until you find the time to make the stock.

Vegetable Stock

Vegetable stocks tend to have less texture than other stocks, as vegetables contain no fat or natural thickeners, such as the collagen found in bones. With a combination of garlic, onions, leeks, and fennel, this stock is a good start for a vegetarian soup. The soup itself can then be fortified with tomatoes or butternut squash for texture, and plenty of fresh herbs for flavor.

2 tablespoons olive oil

4 whole cloves garlic, peeled

2 large Spanish onions, peeled and cut into quarters

2 leeks, washed well and sliced

6 ribs celery, cut into thirds

8 carrots, peeled and cut into thirds

3 parsnips, peeled and cut into thirds

1 bulb fennel, cut into quarters

14 cups water

4 to 6 vegetable bouillon cubes

2 bay leaves

1 tablespoon whole peppercorns

Heat a stockpot over medium-high heat and add the olive oil. Add the garlic, onions, leeks, celery, carrots, parsnips, and fennel. Sauté for 10 minutes, stirring frequently. Add the water, bouillon, bay leaves, and peppercorns. Bring to a boil. Reduce the heat to medium and simmer for 45 minutes. Strain through a fine mesh colander or a regular colander lined with cheesecloth. Discard the solids. Cool to room temperature and refrigerate until ready to use.

Makes 8 cups

First Things First

In generations past, clam broth or consommé made a classy first-course soup, especially when served in bowls set atop monogrammed silver bases. Today's more adventurous appetites call for something less European at the start of a meal. The soups in this chapter are designed to help launch any number of occasions, from a cozy night at home to an elegant holiday dinner. Each one is worthy of its position as the opener for a multi-course meal. Don't expect these soups to stand in for an entrée. They are supposed to whet your appetite and leave you wanting more.

My father was a carpet salesman whose clients included many of the finest hotels around Boston and New England. He seemed to know everyone in the hotel business, and he worked hard at building good relationships with the buyers. Sometimes, he would bring his best clients home for dinner. We learned at an early age how to entertain graciously and make good conversation. When Victor, a buyer from the Sheraton, accepted our dinner invitation, my father was pleased, but also nervous. Dad let us know that Victor was accustomed to eating at fine restaurants, and that he really knew food. My mother suggested consommé because that is what a fine dining restaurant would serve as a first course. We made our own version with tiny cut vegetables. For dessert, we made white chocolate mousse with raspberry sauce. Mom and I thought we were the last word. When Victor called to thank my parents, he commented that he was impressed that we served consommé. This confirmed the success of Mom's strategy—to serve a lovely first-course soup to set the standard for the evening. A good first course inspires confidence that the rest of the meal will follow right along.

Potato-Watercress Soup

Folk wisdom says that watercress can activate a woman's labor. That must be why so many pregnant women stop by our Brookline store after their childbirth classes, held right next door. We enjoy following their progress. Some of these women have even stopped by the store in the throes of labor for their last bowl of soup before they head to the delivery room (how they can manage to eat at such a time, I can't imagine)! The best part is when they bring in their newborns. After that, their children become our customers, too. Just think, we have been feeding them all along!

2 tablespoons butter	2 bunches watercress
1 large Spanish onion, peeled and diced	2 cups light cream
3 ribs celery, diced	4 dashes Worcestershire sauce
3 whole cloves garlic, peeled	3 dashes Tabasco sauce
5 large Yukon Gold potatoes, peeled and cut into 3/4-inch chunks	Kosher salt and freshly ground black pepper, to taste
2 quarts chicken stock	

■ In a stockpot melt the butter over medium-high heat. Add the onion, celery, and garlic. Sauté for 5 to 7 minutes. Add the potatoes and pour in the chicken stock until the potatoes are submerged. Bring to a boil. Reduce the heat to medium high and simmer until the potatoes are tender, 30 to 35 minutes. Remove from the heat and add the watercress. Stir until wilted. Add the cream, Worcestershire sauce, Tabasco sauce, salt, and pepper. Puree the soup in the pot using a hand blender or working in batches with a regular blender until smooth. Return the pot to medium-high heat and simmer for an additional 3 minutes to warm through.

Makes 8 to 10 servings

Vidalia Onion Soup

photo on page 8

It's hard to improve on French onion soup topped with melted cheese that almost magically turns into delicious, gooey strings when you lift a spoon. In this recipe, I wanted to leave the basic concept intact, but find a way to vary the ingredients. Vidalia onions—sometimes called the apple of onions because they are so crunchy and sweet—fit the bill. They grow in a particular area of Georgia, and are the state's official vegetable. When cooked slowly, their sweetness becomes even more pronounced, and they turn a lovely, deep mahogany color. I discovered that sautéing the onions for at least 35 to 40 minutes is the key to giving this soup its rich, slow-cooked flavor. Homey and comforting, this soup can lead off a cozy night at home.

Garlicky Croutons

- 1 French baguette, cut into 15 slices (about 1-inch thick each)
- 2 to 3 tablespoons olive oil
- 1 1/2 teaspoons garlic powder
- 1/2 teaspoon onion powder
- 1/4 teaspoon kosher salt
- 6 grinds of black pepper from a pepper mill

Soup

- 6 tablespoons salted butter
- 8 large Vidalia onions, peeled and sliced
- 3 cloves garlic, peeled and sliced
- 2 cups cream sherry, divided
- 3 tablespoons tomato paste
- 16 cups beef stock
- 2 bay leaves
- 1 tablespoon cornstarch dissolved in 3 tablespoons water
- 1 tablespoon balsamic vinegar
  Kosher salt and freshly ground black pepper, to taste
- 8 to 10 croutons
- 1 1/2 to 2 cups grated Gruyère cheese

■ For the garlicky croutons: Preheat the oven to 350 degrees. Line a baking sheet with parchment paper. In a large mixing bowl toss the bread slices with the olive oil, garlic powder, onion powder, salt, and pepper until the seasonings are evenly distributed. Place on the baking sheet and bake for 8 minutes or until crunchy and hard. Remove from the oven and set aside until ready to use.

■ For the soup: In a stockpot melt the butter over medium heat. Add the onions and sauté for 20 minutes, stirring frequently. Add the garlic and sauté 20 minutes more. Add 1 cup of the sherry. Deglaze the pan, stirring to loosen the cooked pieces on the bottom. Add the remaining 1 cup sherry, tomato paste, beef stock, and bay leaves. Increase the heat to medium-high and bring to a boil. Reduce the heat to medium and simmer for 1 hour. Add the cornstarch-water mixture, increase the heat to high, and boil for 1 minute. Turn off the heat and season with the vinegar, salt, and pepper.

■ Remove and discard the bay leaves.

■ Preheat a broiler to high. Place the soup in an ovenproof casserole or individual crocks. Place the croutons on top of the soup and sprinkle the cheese on top. Broil until the cheese is bubbly and brown, about 3 minutes.

Makes 8 to 10 servings

Leftover Vidalia Onion soup makes a great French dip for sandwiches.

Sweet Potato Soup with Caramelized Onions

We only serve this sweet, creamy soup during the autumn and winter months. Perhaps because of its limited season, it has developed somewhat of a cult following. Its personality comes from the caramelized onions floating in each spoonful. When I make this soup, I always make extra caramelized onions because they make a great topping for whipped potatoes at another meal. The onions can cook while you are preparing the rest of the soup.

The soup makes an elegant first course for a fancy meal. I also used to make a batch for the annual Teacher Appreciation Day luncheon at my daughter's school. I think they gave it an A, because every time I walked into the school, I was greeted with many smiles.

Caramelized Onions

- 2 tablespoons salted butter
- 2 large Spanish onions, peeled and thinly sliced
- 1/2 cup packed dark brown sugar
- Kosher salt and freshly ground black pepper, to taste
- 1/4 cup balsamic vinegar

Soup

- 4 tablespoons salted butter
- 3 whole cloves garlic, peeled and left whole
- 2 cups sliced onions
- 2 cups sliced carrots
- 1/4 cup diced celery
- 8 medium-large sweet potatoes, peeled and cut into chunks
- 10 cups chicken stock
- 1/2 cup packed brown sugar
- 1/2 teaspoon ground nutmeg
- 2 tablespoons Worcestershire sauce
- 2 cups light cream
- 1/2 cup sweet sherry wine
- Kosher salt and freshly ground black pepper, to taste
- 1 1/2 cups caramelized onions

■ For the caramelized onions: In a large sauté pan melt the butter over medium heat. Add the onions and sauté for 18 minutes. Add the brown sugar, salt and pepper. Sauté an additional 10 minutes. Add the vinegar and continue cooking until the vinegar starts to evaporate and the onions look thick and syrupy, 8 to 10 minutes more. Remove from the heat and let cool. If working ahead, the onions can be stored in a tightly covered container until ready to use.

■ For the soup: In a stockpot melt the butter over medium-high heat. Add the garlic, onions, carrots, and celery. Sauté for 10 minutes. Add the sweet potatoes and sauté 5 minutes more. Pour the stock over the vegetables and bring to a boil. Reduce the heat to medium and simmer until the sweet potatoes are very soft, 30 to 35 minutes. Puree the soup in the pot using a hand blender or working in batches with a regular blender until smooth. Add the brown sugar, nutmeg, Worcestershire sauce, light cream, sherry, salt, and pepper. Puree again until well combined. Stir the caramelized onions into the soup with a spoon.

Makes 8 to 10 servings

If you recognize caramel from candy, the technique of caramelizing is related. In candy, sugar is cooked until it liquefies and browns. In this recipe the onions are cooked with sugar and balsamic vinegar in a large sauté pan. All the sugars, including those that occur naturally in the onions and the vinegar, cook down and become syrupy.

Butternut Squash Soup with Calvados, Gorgonzola Cheese, and Prosciutto

Butternut squash looks like a dirty, overgrown pear, but I find it one of the treasures of the fall harvest in New England. Its orange flesh is naturally sweet and goes well with a tremendous variety of ingredients. I came up with this recipe when I was planning to demonstrate my butternut squash-green apple soup recipe on television, and wanted to give it more formality and sophistication. I added Calvados (apple brandy) to cut the sweetness of the squash and the apples. Prosciutto adds a smoky, salty contrast. Gorgonzola dolce, a dessert variation of blue cheese, floats on top, finishing the soup with creaminess as well as pungency.

Garnish

- 1 tablespoon olive oil
- 6 slices prosciutto, cut into thin strips
- 1 green apple, thinly sliced

Soup

- 4 tablespoons butter
- 2 cloves garlic, minced
- 1 1/2 cups diced onions
- 2 large green apples, peeled and diced
- 2 cups diced carrots
- 1/2 cup diced celery
- 1/2 cup diced parsnips
- 2 pounds butternut squash, peeled and diced
- 8 cups chicken stock
  Kosher salt and freshly ground black pepper, to taste
- 1 tablespoon Worcestershire sauce
- 3 tablespoons brown sugar
- 1 1/2 cups light cream
- 2 to 3 tablespoons Calvados
- 8 to 10 tablespoons Gorgonzola dolce cheese

■ **For the garnish:** In a sauté pan heat the olive oil over medium-high heat. Add the prosciutto and pan-fry until crispy. Remove from the pan and set aside. In the same pan, add the apple slices and sauté lightly until crisp-tender. Set aside.

■ **For the soup:** In a stockpot melt the butter over medium-high heat. Add the garlic, onions, apples, carrots, celery, parsnips, and butternut squash. Sauté for 10 minutes. Add the chicken stock and bring to a boil. Reduce the heat to medium and simmer until the vegetables are tender, about 35 minutes.

Puree the soup in the pot using a hand blender or working in batches with a regular blender until smooth. Return the soup to the pot if using a blender and season with salt and pepper, Worcestershire sauce, and brown sugar. Add the cream and stir to incorporate. Return to the heat and simmer for 3 to 5 minutes. Stir in the Calvados right before serving. Top each serving with a dollop of Gorgonzola dolce. Lay slices of sautéed green apple on top. Sprinkle with crispy prosciutto.

Makes 8 to 10 servings

To simplify prep time, buy squash that is already peeled. Many markets sell it this way. The whole squash is only slightly more yielding than a rock, making it difficult to peel with a vegetable peeler, and potentially dangerous to use a sharp knife.

Classic Lobster Bisque

Clam chowder is undoubtedly the signature soup of New England, but lobster bisque is a close second. The early Yankees, ever frugal, used leftover lobster shells to make the stock. We finish our version with a few dashes of Tabasco sauce—just enough to give it some spark without overpowering the lobster flavor. Even though lobster bisque is always served hot, it seems to be most popular during the summer in Boston. At the nearby beaches, where the water is so cold your ankles shiver while your scalp sweats, there is nothing like a mug of hot bisque while you wrap yourself up in a towel to watch the sunset. All summer we pack many quarts of it for people to take to their cottages and boats. Tourists like it, too.

4 tablespoons salted butter	1 cup dry white wine
1 large Spanish onion, peeled and minced	2 cups heavy cream
3 cloves garlic, minced	1 tablespoon Worcestershire sauce
2 carrots, peeled and sliced	1/2 teaspoon Tabasco sauce
2 ribs celery, minced	1 1/4 pounds cooked lobster meat, cut into bite-size pieces
2 large potatoes, peeled and cut into 3/4-inch chunks	1/3 cup brandy or cream sherry
8 cups lobster stock	Kosher salt and freshly ground black pepper, to taste
2 tablespoons tomato paste	

■ In a stockpot melt the butter over medium-high heat. Add the onion, garlic, carrots, and celery. Sauté for 12 minutes. Add the potatoes, lobster stock, tomato paste, and white wine. Bring to a boil. Reduce the heat to medium and simmer until the potatoes are tender and soft, 30 to 35 minutes. Remove from the heat. Puree the soup in the pot using a hand blender or working in batches with a regular blender until very smooth. Stir in the cream, Worcestershire sauce, Tabasco sauce, lobster meat, and brandy or sherry. Season with salt and pepper. Place the pot back on the stove and simmer an additional 3 minutes to heat through.

Makes 8 to 10 servings

Porcini Mushroom Soup

Right before the holidays, we always make giant batches of porcini mushroom soup at our stores. I think of these prized mushrooms as an indulgence that fits perfectly with the holiday theme of celebration. They have a distinctive, deep, woodsy flavor that permeates anything in which they are used. Almost any Christmas dinner entrée can follow a festively-presented bowl of this soup.

3 tablespoons butter	6 cups chicken stock
4 whole cloves garlic, peeled	1 teaspoon dried thyme leaves
1 large Spanish onion, peeled and diced	1/2 cup sherry
2 leeks (white part only), trimmed and sliced	2 cups heavy cream
1 bulb fresh fennel or anise, diced	1/2 teaspoon Worcestershire sauce
3 Yukon Gold potatoes, peeled and cut into 3/4-inch chunks	Kosher salt and freshly ground black pepper, to taste
1 cup dried or 2 pounds fresh porcini mushrooms	

■ In a stockpot melt the butter over medium-high heat. Add the garlic, onion, leeks, and fennel. Sauté for 10 minutes. Add the potatoes, mushrooms, chicken stock, and thyme. Bring to a boil. Reduce the heat to medium and simmer until the potatoes are soft and tender, 30 to 35 minutes. Remove from the heat and add the sherry, cream, Worcestershire sauce, salt, and pepper. Puree with a hand blender or working in batches with a regular blender until smooth. Place the pot back on the stove and simmer an additional 5 to 7 minutes to warm through.

Makes 6 to 8 servings

Fresh porcini mushrooms can be hard to track down and are quite expensive. I have found that dried porcini mushrooms work just as well in this recipe. They can be added right to the soup without presoaking.

Roasted Yellow Pepper and Lobster Soup

We put this soup on the menu every New Year's Eve because it is loaded with symbols of everything I want in the coming year. Its yellow color represents sunshine and brightness. The lobster represents prosperity. The two together are magical. Roasting the peppers brings out their deep, astringent flavor to balance the rich lobster meat. The spices might seem like a surprise, but I think fennel and lobster naturally complement each other, as do ground coriander and bell peppers. The result—a fragrant soup with a luscious texture—always makes me feel like celebrating.

6   to 8 yellow bell peppers

3   tablespoons olive oil

1   large Spanish onion, peeled and diced

4   whole cloves garlic, peeled

3   carrots, peeled and sliced

2   ribs celery, diced

6   cups lobster stock

1   teaspoon fennel seeds

1   tablespoon ground coriander

2   cups light cream

1/4   cup dry vermouth

1   tablespoon Worcestershire sauce

1   tablespoon sherry vinegar

Kosher salt and freshly ground black pepper, to taste

2   cups cooked lobster meat, cut into bite-size pieces

Freshly snipped chives, for garnish

■ Preheat the oven to 425 degrees. Line a baking sheet with aluminum foil or parchment paper. Place the whole peppers on top. Bake, turning the peppers once or twice, until the skins are black and charred, 30 to 35 minutes. Remove from the oven and immediately place the peppers (use tongs or a fork to avoid burning yourself) in a paper bag and close the top. Let them sit for 15 minutes. Unwrap the bag and remove the peppers. Peel away and discard the skin (it should slip right off at this point). Cut the peppers in half and remove the seeds. Set aside.

■ Heat a stock pot over medium-high heat and add the olive oil. Add the onions, garlic, carrots, and celery. Sauté for 10 minutes. Add the roasted peppers, lobster stock, fennel seeds, and coriander. Bring to a boil and let simmer for 30 minutes. Puree the soup in the pot using a hand blender or working in batches with a regular blender until smooth. Add the cream, vermouth, Worcestershire sauce, vinegar, salt and pepper. Add the lobster meat and stir to combine. Garnish with freshly snipped chives.

Makes 8 to 10 servings

Tomato Teasers

Tomatoes are the better half of any soup. Their bold, acidic flavor helps balance other elements in the pot. Somehow they manage to give everything a robust undertone and an uplifting taste. They easily pair with a surprising range of ingredients, from shrimp to fennel. These recipes highlight tomatoes in a simple soup with rice; a summery mix with corn and basil; an aromatic, Asian-inspired blend with ginger and chicken; and many vegetarian selections.

Early in our marriage, Paul and I rented a home near my parents. We were so excited because it had a yard and we could plant our first garden. Though the house was falling apart, the soil was incredibly fertile. We went to a garden center and bought as many fruit and vegetable plants as we could find. We spent the weekend digging and planting, but we soon realized that we were running out of space.

Paul started to dig some more holes in the backyard when all of a sudden the next door neighbor came flying out the door, waving his arms and screaming. His name was Al, and nobody in the neighborhood spoke to him because he had a reputation for being mean and grumpy. His behavior now was no exception. "Who the hell do you think you are?" he shouted. "That's my land you're digging into, not yours."

Paul apologized and told him that he would remove the plants if Al insisted, but we would share our vegetables and fruits with him if he let us keep them there. Al angrily told Paul he could leave the plants, but to remember that it is was his land.

When August had finally arrived, our fragrant tomatoes were ripening next to a patch of basil. We feasted on everything we had planted, and there was plenty to share with Al.

After about a year, Paul noticed that Al's lawn was growing too tall and that it needed to be mowed. Before then, he had always kept it perfectly groomed. So the next time that Paul mowed our lawn, he did Al's, too. One day, Al came out of his house looking haggard. He told us he had cancer and he was too weak to mow his lawn. He thanked Paul for doing it for him. When our daughter was born the following spring, Al brought us a beautifully wrapped gift. He was so excited for us, but we could see that he was deteriorating. Later that year, he died from his cancer. How grateful we were that planting too many tomatoes had blossomed into a beautiful friendship.

Tomato-Parsnip Soup

One morning as I paced the kitchen floor dreaming up my next big idea for tomato soup, someone delivered a 50-pound bag of parsnips. That's all the inspiration I needed. Before I even gave myself time to figure out how the tomatoes would taste with parsnips, I was putting together the soup. The parsnips actually steal the show, mellowing the acidity of the tomatoes with their mild, earthy flavor. This vegetarian soup is both hearty and comforting.

3   tablespoons olive oil
4   whole cloves garlic, peeled
1   large Spanish onion, peeled and diced
2   ribs celery, sliced
12 to 15 parsnips, peeled and sliced
6   cups whole peeled tomatoes (canned or fresh)

2   cups tomato juice
4   cups vegetable stock or water
2   cups light cream
3   tablespoons chopped fresh dill
    Kosher salt and freshly ground black pepper, to taste

■ Heat a heavy, lined stockpot over medium-high heat. Add the olive oil, garlic, onion, celery, and parsnips. Sauté for 10 minutes. Add the tomatoes, tomato juice, and vegetable stock. Bring to a boil. Reduce the heat to a simmer and cook until the parsnips are soft and tender, 35 to 40 minutes. Remove from the heat. Puree the soup in the pot using a hand blender or working in batches with a regular blender until smooth. Return the soup to the pot and add the cream, dill, salt, and pepper.

Makes 10 to 12 servings

Yellow Tomato Soup with Jasmine Rice

Making the effort to find locally-grown tomatoes is the key to this soup's success. Yellow tomatoes are nice and meaty, and a little less acidic than other varieties. This soup stays on our menu all summer long. The rice adds body to the vegetables.

12 large yellow tomatoes

3 tablespoons extra-virgin olive oil

3 whole cloves garlic, peeled

2 cups diced onions

1/2 cup diced celery

2 cups diced carrots

10 sun-dried tomatoes, packed in oil

2 quarts chicken or vegetable stock

2 cups V-8 juice

1 bunch fresh basil leaves

1 tablespoon sherry vinegar

1 tablespoon Worcestershire sauce

Kosher salt and freshly ground black pepper, to taste

3 cups cooked jasmine rice

■ Bring a pot of water to a boil. With a small paring knife cut an X into the bottom of each tomato. Drop the tomatoes, 2 or 3 at a time, into the boiling water. Leave for 30 seconds. Remove and rinse with cold water. Remove the skin by pulling the X shape from the bottom of the tomato. Set aside.

■ Heat a stockpot over medium-high heat. Add the olive oil, garlic, onions, celery, carrots, peeled tomatoes, and sun-dried tomatoes. Sauté for 10 minutes. Add the stock and V-8 juice. Bring to a boil. Reduce the heat to medium and simmer for 30 minutes. Remove from the heat and add the basil, vinegar, Worcestershire sauce, salt, and pepper. Puree the soup in the pot using a hand blender or working in batches with a regular blender until smooth. Add the rice and stir well to incorporate.

Makes 12 servings

Turn this soup into a summer entrée by grilling some shrimp or scallops and placing them on top. A tossed salad made from seasonal greens and chopped fresh herbs could complete the meal. On the side, serve slices of French bread that you brush with olive oil and toast on the grill.

Roasted Tomato and Rice Soup

This soup has all of the classic components of tomato and rice soup, but the flavor becomes deeper and more concentrated because the tomatoes are roasted. The oven truly brings out their hidden flavors. I like to use plum tomatoes because they are sturdy enough to stand up well to roasting. You don't even have to peel them first.

Roasted Tomatoes

- 12 plum tomatoes, cut into halves
- 3 tablespoons olive oil

  Kosher salt and freshly ground black pepper, to taste

Soup

- 3 tablespoons butter
- 3 whole cloves garlic, peeled
- 1 large Spanish onion, peeled and diced
- 5 carrots, peeled and sliced
- 2 ribs celery, sliced

Roasted plum tomatoes (from recipe)

- 6 sun-dried tomatoes, packed in oil
- 6 cups vegetable or chicken stock
- 3 cups tomato juice
- 2 tablespoons chopped fresh basil
- 2 1/2 cups cooked white rice
- 4 dashes Worcestershire sauce

  Kosher salt and freshly ground black pepper, to taste
- 1 1/2 to 2 cups grated sharp cheddar cheese

  Croutons, for garnish (from Vidalia Onion Soup recipe on page 12)

■ For the roasted tomatoes: Preheat the oven to 425 degrees. Place the tomatoes in a small roasting pan. Toss with the olive oil, salt, and pepper. Place in the oven and roast for 50 minutes, or until the skins look wrinkled but the tomatoes retain their shape.

■ For the soup: In a stockpot melt the butter over medium-high heat. Add the garlic, onion, carrots, and celery. Sauté for 10 minutes, stirring frequently. Add the roasted tomatoes and continue to sauté for 5 minutes. Add the sun-dried tomatoes, stock, and tomato juice.

Bring to a boil. Reduce the heat to medium. Simmer, covered, for 30 minutes. Add the basil. Puree the soup in the pot using a hand blender or working in batches with a regular blender until smooth. Place the soup back into the pot if using a regular blender. Add the rice and season with Worcestershire sauce, salt, and pepper. Stir so that the rice is evenly distributed throughout the soup. Sprinkle each serving with cheese and croutons.

Makes 10 servings

Instead of serving a grilled cheese sandwich on the side, garnish the soup with freshly grated, sharp cheddar cheese and crisp croutons. You get the same cheese flavor and toasty crunch in a more interesting presentation.

Tomato, Corn, and Basil Soup

One steamy summer afternoon, I came home from work to a countertop filled with extremely ripe tomatoes. I pulled out the stockpot and proceeded to make a batch of this soup. Just as I was finishing, the doorbell rang. It was my sister, Janie, and her family dropping off some clothes they had borrowed. She couldn't understand why I would come home and make a pot of soup in 87-degree heat. I'm totally infatuated with soup, and I couldn't let those tomatoes, which come around only once a year, go to waste.

3 tablespoons butter or olive oil

2 large Spanish onions, peeled and diced

5 carrots, peeled and sliced

2 ribs celery, sliced

4 cloves garlic, minced

8 large, ripe, red tomatoes, peeled and cut into chunks (see note)

8 cups vegetable or chicken stock

3 cups tomato juice

1 can (6 ounces) tomato paste

2 teaspoons sugar

1 bunch chopped fresh basil leaves

1 tablespoon balsamic vinegar

Kernels from 5 ears corn

Kosher salt and freshly ground black pepper, to taste

■ In a stockpot heat the butter or olive oil over medium-high heat. Add the onions, carrots, celery, and garlic. Sauté for 10 minutes, stirring frequently. Add the tomatoes and sauté an additional 5 minutes. Add the stock, tomato juice, and tomato paste. Bring to a boil. Reduce the heat to medium and simmer, covered, for 25 to 30 minutes, or until all of the vegetables are soft and tender.

Add the sugar, fresh basil, and vinegar.

Puree the soup in the pot using a hand blender or working in batches with a regular blender until smooth. Add the corn kernels to the soup and return the pot to medium-high heat. Simmer for an additional 5 to 7 minutes until the corn is cooked and the soup is heated through. Season with salt and pepper.

Makes 12 servings

For directions on peeling tomatoes see Yellow Tomato Soup with Jasmine Rice on page 29.

Tomato, Butternut Squash, and Herb Soup

When I set out to make a tomato soup that wasn't too acidic, I discovered that butternut squash was the wonder ingredient I needed for balance. The squash has a hint of sweetness, plus a starchy consistency to give the soup a luscious thickness. The healthy combination of vegetables keeps customers steadily ordering this soup all year long. The butternut squash offers a mega-dose of Vitamin A (one cup of cubed squash contains nearly 300 percent of your daily requirement), and the tomatoes are high in Vitamin C. After this, I experimented with adding butternut squash to lots of other soups. No matter how many other variations I dream up, squash with tomato remains a winning combination.

3	tablespoons butter
3	whole cloves garlic, peeled
1	large Spanish onion, peeled and diced
5	carrots, peeled and sliced
2	ribs celery, diced
2	pounds butternut squash, peeled and cut into large chunks
2	cans (14 ounces each) whole tomatoes
8	cups vegetable or chicken stock
1	cup sherry
1/2	cup chopped fresh basil leaves
1/2	cup chopped fresh cilantro leaves
1	tablespoon balsamic vinegar
	Kosher salt and freshly ground black pepper, to taste

In a stockpot melt the butter over medium-high heat. Add the garlic, onion, carrots, celery, and butternut squash. Sauté for 10 minutes. Add the tomatoes, stock, and sherry. Bring to a boil. Reduce the heat to medium, cover the pot, and simmer until the squash is tender and soft, 35 to 40 minutes. Remove from the heat and add the basil, cilantro, vinegar, salt, and pepper. Puree in the pot using a hand blender or in a regular blender working in batches until smooth.

Makes 12 servings

Since vegetarian soups aren't fortified by the proteins found in meat or fish stocks, their texture tends to be a bit thinner. Pureed butternut squash makes a tasty, natural thickener.

Tomato, Shrimp, and Fennel Soup

photo on page 24

In soup, I find that fennel complements the flavors and textures of tomatoes and shrimp.

Roasted Fennel

3   bulbs fresh fennel, chopped and stems discarded

2   to 3 tablespoons extra-virgin olive oil
    Kosher salt and freshly ground black pepper, to taste

Soup

3   tablespoons olive oil

4   whole cloves garlic, peeled

1   large Spanish onion, diced

2   ribs celery, diced

2   carrots, peeled and sliced

6   cups peeled whole tomatoes (canned or fresh)

4   cups fish or chicken stock

1   tablespoon fennel seeds

1   pound uncooked small shrimp, peeled and deveined

2   tablespoons extra-virgin olive oil

1   tablespoon balsamic vinegar

8   to 10 leaves fresh basil, torn
    Kosher salt and freshly ground black pepper, to taste

■ For the roasted fennel: Preheat the oven to 425 degrees. Place the fennel in a small roasting pan and drizzle with olive oil. Season with salt and pepper. Bake for 25 minutes, or until the edges turn a light caramel color.

■ For the soup: Heat the olive oil in a large, heavy-bottomed stockpot over medium-high heat. Sauté the garlic, onions, celery, and carrots for 10 minutes. Add the tomatoes, stock, and fennel seeds. Bring to a boil.

Reduce the heat to medium low and simmer for 30 minutes. Remove from the heat. Puree the soup in the pot using a hand blender or working in batches with a regular blender until smooth. Return to the heat. Add the shrimp and cook for 3 to 5 minutes. Add the roasted fennel, olive oil, vinegar, basil, salt, and pepper. Return to the stove and heat an additional 2 minutes.

Makes 12 servings

Tomato and Ginger Soup with Grilled Chicken

While growing up in Boston, my family and I frequently visited Chinatown to explore the restaurants. One of our favorites was Carl's Pagoda. It was an unassuming place with outdated décor, but the food was something else. You would not normally expect a Chinese restaurant to serve tomato soup, but Carl's made it a specialty. It had a real gingery taste that was clean and pungent.

The first time that I tried to recreate this soup, I had just finished grilling marinated chicken for our salads, and decided to add some. It worked beautifully, and people thought the soup had such a unique flavor that I decided to keep making it with the chicken. When I brought the soup to the "Phantom Gourmet" television show in Boston, the show's producers and hosts, brothers Dan and Dave Andelman, also remembered the Carl's Pagoda soup from their childhood.

Chicken

1 tablespoon minced fresh ginger

3 cloves garlic, minced

1/4 cup soy sauce

1 tablespoon ketchup

1 tablespoon honey

1 tablespoon rice wine vinegar

2 whole (about 1 pound each) boneless, skinless chicken breasts

Soup

3 tablespoons peanut oil

4 cloves garlic, chopped

3 tablespoons minced fresh ginger

2 large Spanish onions, peeled and diced

2 ribs celery, sliced

4 carrots, peeled and sliced

2 cans (28 ounce each) whole tomatoes

2 teaspoons dried coriander

1/2 teaspoon crushed red pepper flakes

6 cups chicken stock

2 cups sherry

3 tablespoons soy sauce

1 tablespoon rice wine vinegar

2 tablespoons chopped fresh cilantro
Kosher salt and freshly ground black pepper, to taste

■ For the chicken: In a large glass or ceramic bowl, mix the ginger, garlic, soy sauce, ketchup, honey, and vinegar. Add the chicken breasts and stir until completely coated with the marinade. Cover and place in the refrigerator overnight.

■ Preheat a grill or broiler. Remove the chicken from the marinade and grill or broil until cooked through, about 6 minutes per side. When cool enough to handle, cut into thin slices. Set aside.

■ For the soup: Heat a large stockpot over medium-high heat and add the peanut oil. Add the garlic, ginger, onions, celery, and carrots. Sauté for 10 minutes. Add the tomatoes, coriander, red pepper flakes, stock, and sherry. Bring to a boil. Reduce the heat slightly and simmer, covered, for 35 minutes. Add the soy sauce, vinegar, and cilantro. Puree with a regular blender or hand blender until smooth. Return the soup to the pot if using a regular blender. Season with salt and pepper and add the slices of chicken breast.

Makes 8 to 10 servings

When making this recipe, don't be tempted to substitute ginger powder, as the fresh ginger root is essential to the flavor. Since ginger grows in large clumps, you'll probably be purchasing a piece of a root. Look for unwrinkled skin and an unblemished end where it was snapped off the larger root. Peel off the tough, outer layer of skin before using.

Say Cheese, Please

Cheese usually makes a soup taste even better by adding salty richness and depth. Each cheese has its own flavor and its own properties for melting into a soup. Many ingredients take on a new personality when paired with cheese. I use this to my advantage to build soups from spinach and feta; artichokes and Parmesan; and beets, pears, and blue cheese. For fun, I even found a way to make a soup from eggplant Parmesan ingredients. It really does taste like a liquid version of the real thing.

Gorgonzola cheese, made in Italy, is one of the tastiest of the blue-veined cheeses. Yet I was initially reluctant to use it in my soups because its strong aroma kept reminding me of a mistake I made during my earlier days as a caterer. I was equal parts ambition, bravado, and inexperience—sometimes a disastrous combination. Wanting to show my sophisticated tastes, I suggested that a client giving a graduation party dispense with the usual assortment of cheese and crackers and serve a big wheel of Gorgonzola cheese surrounded by fresh cherries and other stone fruits.

Too bad it was about 85 degrees outside on the day of the party, and the client had no air conditioning. She did have two fans, which she placed at either end of the living room, while her big dog barked at me. When I set out the wheel of cheese, the odor blew everywhere! My great idea for a centerpiece had turned into a smelly fiasco. I wanted to hide in the kitchen. It took me several years before I could look at the cheese again. Only after reminding myself that I really did like Gorgonzola in the first place was I able to cook with it again.

Spinach, Feta Cheese, and Toasted Pine Nut Soup

When I was growing up, I was probably the only kid in town who actually asked if I could just finish my spinach instead of eating a slice of cake for dessert. So I was always thrilled when the Greek Orthodox Church across the street from my house served spanakopita, a pastry filled with spinach and feta cheese, at its annual food festivals. I knew that one of these festivals had started when I detected the aroma on my way home from school. After stopping at home for some money, I would rush into the church, where about 12 different ladies sold their own homemade spinach and cheese pies. I never wanted to make a bad impression, so I tried to buy a piece from each one during the three days of the festival. This soup is a tribute to the women who introduced me to the simple joy of combining spinach with feta cheese.

3 tablespoons butter

4 whole cloves garlic, peeled

1 large Spanish onion, peeled and diced

3 ribs celery, diced

4 large Yukon Gold potatoes, peeled and cut into chunks

6 cups vegetable or chicken stock

1 cup white wine

1/2 teaspoon ground nutmeg

2 pounds fresh spinach leaves

2 cups light cream

1 cup crumbled feta cheese (reserve about 1/4 cup, for garnish)

1/4 cup pine nuts, toasted (reserve a few, for garnish)

4 dashes Worcestershire sauce

Kosher salt and freshly ground black pepper, to taste

41

In a stockpot melt the butter over medium-high heat. Add the garlic, onion, and celery. Sauté for 5 minutes. Add the potatoes and sauté for an additional 5 minutes. Add the stock and wine. Bring to a boil. Reduce the heat to medium and simmer until the potatoes are soft and tender, 30 to 35 minutes. Add the nutmeg and spinach. Stir until the spinach wilts into the soup. Remove from the heat. Puree the soup in the pot using a hand blender or working in batches with a regular blender until smooth. Stir in the cream, cheese, pine nuts, Worcestershire sauce, salt, and pepper. Return the pot to the stove and simmer an additional 5 minutes. Garnish each serving with crumbled feta cheese and a few toasted pine nuts.

Makes 10 servings

Pine nuts, called pignoli in Italy, are harvested from the cones of certain varieties of pine trees. Toasting greatly enhances their flavor. The best method for doing this is to preheat the oven to 350 degrees and line a baking sheet with foil or parchment paper. Spread the nuts in a single layer and bake for 5 to 7 minutes, stirring once so they toast evenly. Watch carefully because they burn easily.

Artichoke Bisque

photo on page 38

Artichokes have been considered a delicacy—and an aphrodisiac—since ancient Greece. Maybe that is why Marilyn Monroe was crowned the Queen of Artichokes in 1947. Very few people know how to cook with artichokes, but they always seem to like them. I'm one of those people who is patient enough to let an artichoke steam for at least thirty minutes, then pull it apart, leaf by leaf, dipping the base of each one in Hollandaise sauce.

This recipe is based on canned artichoke hearts, which give you an instant artichoke fix. It produces a pale green, decadent blend of flavors and textures. One of our regular customers enters our store blurting out, "Artichoke bisque today?" When we tell her it's on the menu, she always orders a large container.

Roasted Artichoke Garnish

1 can (16 ounces) artichoke hearts, drained and cut into small pieces

1 tablespoon olive oil

1 clove garlic, minced

Kosher salt and freshly ground black pepper, to taste

Soup

4 tablespoons salted butter

2 cups sliced onions

4 whole cloves garlic, peeled

1/4 cup diced celery

6 Yukon Gold potatoes, peeled and cut into quarters

3 cans (16 ounces each) artichoke hearts, drained

8 cups chicken stock

2 cups freshly grated Parmesan cheese

1/2 teaspoon ground nutmeg

Kosher salt and freshly ground black pepper, to taste

8 to 10 dashes Tabasco sauce

2 teaspoons Worcestershire sauce

2 cups light cream

Roasted artichokes (from recipe)

2 tablespoons chopped fresh parsley

For the roasted artichoke garnish: Preheat the oven to 400 degrees. In a mixing bowl, combine the artichoke hearts, olive oil, garlic, salt, and pepper. Place this mixture into an 8-inch square roasting pan and bake for 12 to 15 minutes until the edges of the artichokes turn a light, crispy brown. Set aside.

For the soup: In a stockpot melt the butter. Add the onions, garlic, and celery. Sauté for 15 minutes until the onions start to caramelize a bit. Add the potatoes and artichoke hearts and stir together to incorporate. Pour the chicken stock over the ingredients and bring to a boil over medium-high heat. Reduce the heat to medium and simmer until the potatoes are soft and tender, 30 to 35 minutes. Puree the soup in the pot using a hand blender or working in batches with a regular blender until the ingredients are well mixed. Add the cheese, nutmeg, salt, pepper, Tabasco sauce, and Worcestershire sauce. Puree once again until the ingredients are well mixed. Add the cream and puree until the entire soup is smooth. Serve in colorful bowls. Garnish each serving with roasted artichokes and fresh parsley sprinkled in the center.

Makes 6 to 8 servings

Stock your pantry with canned artichoke hearts so you can make this soup on the spur of the moment. You are more likely to have the other key ingredients—potatoes, onions, chicken stock, Parmesan cheese, and light cream—on hand.

Roasted Yellow Beet and Pear Soup with Crumbled Blue Cheese

After visiting my local Farmers' Market one September day, I dumped the contents of my canvas tote bags on my kitchen table and decided to see if I could make a soup from the vegetables. I thought that beets and pears would go well together, since both reach the peak of their season around the same time. Roasting the beets brings out their natural sweetness and earthy flavor. This lovely, lemon-colored soup can be served hot or cold, which perfectly suits the fickle New England weather in late September.

Roasted Beets

- 3 bunches fresh yellow beets, washed and stems trimmed
- 2 tablespoons olive oil
  Kosher salt, as needed

Soup

- 3 tablespoons salted butter
- 2 whole cloves garlic, peeled
- 1 large Spanish onion, peeled and diced
- 2 ribs celery, diced
- 1 large carrot, peeled and sliced
- 4 to 5 large ripe pears, peeled, seeded, and quartered

- 3 bunches roasted beets
- 8 cups chicken stock
- 1/2 cup vermouth
- 2 tablespoons honey
- 1 tablespoon apple cider vinegar
- 1 cup sour cream
- 1 cup light cream
  Kosher salt and freshly ground black pepper, to taste
- 1 to 2 thinly sliced pears, for garnish
- 3/4 cup crumbled blue cheese, for garnish

For the roasted beets: Preheat the oven to 450 degrees. Place the beets on a large piece of foil. Rub the beets with the oil and sprinkle on all sides with salt. Loosely close the foil and place in a roasting pan. Bake for 1 hour, or until the beets can be easily pierced with a fork. Remove and let cool just until they can be handled. Peel and discard the skins. Set aside.

For the soup: In a stockpot melt the butter over medium-high heat. Add the garlic, onion, celery, carrot, and quartered pears. Sauté for 10 minutes. Add the roasted beets, chicken stock, and vermouth (the liquid should cover the beets). Bring to a boil. Reduce the heat to medium and simmer for 30 minutes. Remove from the stove and puree the soup in the pot using a hand blender or working in batches with a regular blender until the ingredients are well mixed. Add the honey, vinegar, sour cream, light cream, salt, and pepper. Puree once again until smooth. Garnish each serving with pear slices and blue cheese.

Makes 8 to 10 servings

Except for a pick-your-own place, you will never find a fresher and more colorful assortment of vegetables, honey, eggs, and flowers than at a Farmers' Market. At my local market near Boston, farmers drive in once a week to sell whatever they have harvested earlier that day. I try to rearrange my schedule just so that I never miss one of their visits. The array of fresh ingredients, some of which are still covered with dirt, can be an inspiration, and the quality tends to be infinitely better than plastic-wrapped produce from the supermarket.

Cauliflower, Potato, and Cheese Soup

Forget the saying that too many cooks spoil the broth. A professional kitchen relies on teamwork to keep things running smoothly. Chef Ted Colozzi has been helping us orchestrate the daily operations of our kitchen for close to eight years. We graduated from culinary school together back in the 1980s, and we always share tips with each other. In addition to having great taste, Chef Ted is one of the nicest people I have ever known. This soup is his favorite from our entire menu. The potatoes give the soup its wonderful thickness, and the sharp cheese gives it a bite. Its creamy, cheesy consistency holds up beautifully on a spoon. On a chilly Saturday afternoon, serve it with griddled Black Forest Ham Sandwiches on pumpernickel bread (see page 204) for a twist on basic ham and cheese.

Garnish (optional)

- 1 cup cauliflower florets
- 1 tablespoon olive oil
- Kosher salt, to taste

Soup

- 2 tablespoons salted butter
- 2 whole cloves garlic, peeled
- 3 cups diced onions
- 1 cup diced celery
- 2 heads cauliflower, separated into florets
- 3 Yukon Gold potatoes, peeled and cut into chunks
- 10 cups chicken stock
- 4 cups shredded sharp cheddar cheese
- 2 cups light cream
- 1 teaspoon ground nutmeg
- 1 teaspoon dry mustard
- 3 teaspoons Worcestershire sauce
- 6 dashes Tabasco sauce
- Kosher salt and freshly ground black pepper, to taste

For the garnish: Preheat the oven to 375 degrees. In a mixing bowl, toss the cauliflower florets with the olive oil and salt. Place in an 8-inch square roasting pan and bake for 20 minutes, or until the cauliflower has softened and has a roasted, brown exterior. Set aside.

For the soup: In a stockpot melt the butter over medium-high heat. Add the garlic, onions, celery, cauliflower florets, and potatoes. Sauté for 10 minutes. Add enough stock to cover the vegetables and bring to a boil. Reduce the heat to medium and simmer until the potatoes are tender, 30 to 35 minutes. Remove from the heat. Add the cheese, cream, nutmeg, mustard, Worcestershire sauce, Tabasco sauce, salt, and pepper. Puree the soup in the pot using a hand blender or working in batches with a regular blender until smooth. Garnish each serving with a few roasted cauliflower florets.

Makes 8 to 10 servings

Eggplant Parmesan Soup

Eggplant Parmesan is one of my favorite things to eat, so I couldn't resist turning it into a soup. This recipe has all of the components of the beloved casserole—and tastes exactly like it—but you can eat it with a spoon. It's healthier, too, because the eggplant is not fried.

2 large (approximately 1 to 1¼ pounds each) purple eggplants	1 cup white wine
3 tablespoons olive oil	1 teaspoon dried oregano
3 cloves garlic, minced	1 teaspoon dried basil
1 large Spanish onion, peeled and diced	4 cups garlic croutons (from Vidalia Onion Soup recipe on page 12)
2 ribs celery, diced	2 cups shredded Parmesan cheese
1¼ cups canned stewed tomatoes	1 tablespoon balsamic vinegar
2 cups tomato juice	Kosher salt and freshly ground black pepper, to taste
8 cups vegetable stock	

■ Preheat the oven to 425 degrees. Wash the eggplants and pat dry. With a fork prick each one in several places. Place on a roasting pan or baking sheet and place in the oven. Roast for 35 to 40 minutes, or until soft. Remove from the oven and let cool slightly. Over a mixing bowl, peel back the skin and use a spoon or your hands to remove all of the pulp. Discard the skin. Place the pulp, a small amount at a time, onto a cutting board and chop into small pieces. (Don't worry about its appearance. It is supposed to look wet and a bit mushy). Return to the mixing bowl and set aside.

■ Heat a stockpot over medium-high heat. Add the olive oil, garlic, onion, and celery. Sauté for 10 minutes, stirring frequently. Add the eggplant pulp, tomatoes, tomato juice, stock, wine, oregano, and basil. Bring to a boil. Reduce the heat to medium and simmer for 35 minutes.

 While the soup is simmering, place the croutons in the bowl of a food processor and process them into breadcrumbs. Set aside.

 To finish the soup, add the cheese, stirring while it melts. Add the vinegar, salt, and pepper, and stir well. Stir in the breadcrumbs. Simmer an additional 5 to 7 minutes before serving.

Makes 8 to 10 servings

Potato, Crab, and Gorgonzola Soup

At first, blue cheese and crab might not seem like the most likely pairing of ingredients. Yet this combination works quite well because gorgonzola is mild enough not to overpower the more delicate crab. Added in the final stages of preparation, the cheese balances the mild potatoes and the rich, salty crabmeat with just the right pungency. Make this rich soup when you want a luxurious treat.

3   tablespoons butter

4   whole cloves garlic, peeled

1   large Spanish onion, peeled and diced

3   ribs celery, diced

6   large Yukon Gold potatoes, peeled and cut into chunks

6   cups lobster stock

1   can (8 ounces) tomato paste

2   cups sherry

2   bay leaves

1   teaspoon celery salt

2   cups heavy cream

1   pound cooked crabmeat

1   cup crumbled Gorgonzola cheese (reserve about 1/4 cup, for garnish)

1/2   bunch chopped fresh basil (reserve about 1 tablespoon, for garnish)

5   dashes Worcestershire sauce

4   dashes Tabasco sauce

    Kosher salt and freshly ground black pepper, to taste

In a stockpot melt the butter over medium-high heat. Add the garlic, onion, and celery. Sauté for 5 minutes. Add the potatoes and cook an additional 5 minutes. Add the lobster stock, tomato paste, sherry, bay leaves, and celery salt. Bring to a boil. Reduce the heat to medium and simmer until the potatoes are soft and tender, 30 to 35 minutes.

Remove and discard the bay leaves. Remove from the heat and add the cream. Puree the soup in the pot using a hand blender or working in batches with a regular blender until smooth and creamy. Add the crabmeat, cheese, basil, Worcestershire sauce, Tabasco sauce, salt, and pepper. Stir well. Return the pot to the heat and simmer for an additional 5 minutes, adding a bit more sherry, to taste. Garnish each serving with the crumbled cheese, any extra crabmeat, and chopped basil.

Makes 10 servings

Not all blue cheeses are created equal. Though they all contain an edible form of mold that gives them their distinctive blue, veiny appearance, their flavor can range from mild to intensely pungent. Gorgonzola, made in Italy, falls on the mild end of the scale.

A Chicken in Every Pot

Think of chicken as a miracle ingredient for soup. Its rich, golden color and flavor form the base for a vast menu, from clear broth to gumbo. A simple chicken soup made with carrots, celery, and onions soothes and nourishes you to the core. No wonder this is sometimes called "Jewish penicillin." The recipes in this chapter include comfort food as well as a Caribbean one with coconut and lime. There's even a spicy flu chaser, the result of a customer's psychic vision. If a bowl of that doesn't banish whatever ails you, call the doctor!

Over the years, customers have suggested many different ideas for soups, but never with the certainty of the man who one day told me I had a special ability to invent a soup that would heal people. I had never seen him before he and his wife came in for lunch three days in a row. They were both suffering from horrible colds. On the third day, when I struck up a conversation, they told me that my chicken soup and my sweet and sour cabbage soup were the only thing that made them feel better. I thanked them and returned to wait on other customers. About ten minutes later, the man walked back up to me and told me he is a gifted psychic. "I feel your energy and it is very good," he said. "The spirit is telling me that you need to invent a soup that can make people feel better."

Mystified but also captivated by his message, I got right to work the next day. I knew that the base of the soup would be homemade chicken stock, because what could be better to start with than so-called Jewish penicillin? Grandmother Florrie always raved about how ginger helped upset stomachs, so I knew that would be another ingredient. Hot lemonade, my parents' home remedy, prompted me to put in lemon juice. Next came garlic, rumored to ward off evil spirits. The soup grew as I thought about every ingredient that might have healing powers. When I was done, I guess something powerful was on my side. I tasted the broth and thought it was just right. It had all of the elements needed to nurse someone back to health. Who needs a Jewish grandmother when you have a soup doctor?

Caribbean Chicken Soup with Coconut

This chicken soup is memorable because it manages to be simultaneously hot, tangy, and slightly sweet, with chewy bits of coconut floating in it. It has just as many healing qualities as traditional chicken soup, maybe even more, thanks to the ginger, which is supposed to aid digestion. I find myself making this soup most during the spring and summer, as it has a wonderful tropical feel.

3 tablespoons canola oil	12 cups chicken stock
5 cloves garlic, minced	Juice and zest of 3 limes
2 tablespoons peeled and minced fresh ginger	1 can (14 1/2 ounces) coconut milk
1 large Spanish onion, peeled and diced	2 teaspoons ground coriander
2 ribs celery, diced	1/2 teaspoon allspice
4 carrots, peeled and sliced	8 dashes hot sauce, preferably Melinda's brand XXX habanero sauce
1 large red bell pepper, diced	1 bunch chopped fresh cilantro
2 cups chopped cooked chicken meat	Kosher salt and freshly ground black pepper, to taste
1 1/2 cups whole corn kernels	
1 cup shredded coconut	

In a stockpot over medium-high heat add the oil, garlic, ginger, onion, celery, carrots, and red pepper. Sauté for 5 minutes. Add the chicken, corn, coconut, and stock. Bring to a boil. Reduce the heat to medium and simmer for 30 minutes. Add the lime juice and zest, coconut milk, coriander, allspice, hot sauce, cilantro, salt, and pepper. Simmer an additional 5 minutes.

Makes 10 to 12 servings

If you can't get away for a winter vacation, but crave something tropical, make this soup. It goes really well with a few pieces of freshly made cornbread. To order Melinda's XXXtra Hot Sauce order go to www.melindas.com or call 800-886-6354.

Grandma Florrie's Chicken Soup with Matzo Balls

photo on page 54

When I was growing up, almost everything that came out of my Grandma Florrie's kitchen tasted like perfection to me. Though she was elegant, proper, and sophisticated, she liked nothing more than a cooking project. She was one of the first people I knew to own a Cuisinart. From her home in Detroit, she traveled all over the world, sometimes writing down her recipes on cruise ship stationery. I could always count on her to order exotic foods, such as Rainier cherries or Iranian pistachios. When she passed away, I inherited all her recipes, pots, and pans. I attribute much of my love of food to her influence. Grandma Florrie was proud of her chicken soup, and always made it the same way. She swore that using a veal bone and a sweet potato were the secrets to its success. I have to agree. Whipped egg whites and club soda helped make her matzo balls nice and light.

Matzo Balls

- 7 eggs, separated
- 1 tablespoon kosher salt, divided
- 1/4 cup chicken fat or vegetable oil, such as canola
- 1 3/4 cups matzo meal
- 2 1/2 tablespoons club soda
- 2 teaspoons onion powder
- 1 tablespoon chopped fresh parsley

Soup

- 3 pounds chicken thighs
- 1 veal bone
- 2 large Spanish onions, peeled and diced
- 4 ribs celery, diced
- 10 carrots, peeled and sliced
- 2 gallons water, plus additional as needed
  Kosher salt, to taste
- 3 sweet potatoes, peeled and diced
- 1 bunch chopped fresh dill
- 2 tablespoons chopped fresh parsley

For the matzo balls: Fill an 8-quart pot three-quarters of the way with salted water or chicken stock. Bring to a boil over high heat.

Place the egg whites in a mixing bowl and add a pinch of salt. Using an electric mixer, whip the egg whites until stiff peaks form. Set aside.

In a separate bowl mix together the egg yolks, remaining salt, chicken fat, matzo meal, club soda, onion powder, and parsley. Gently fold the egg whites into the batter. Place in the refrigerator for 15 minutes. Using your hands roll the batter into walnut-size pieces. Drop the matzo balls into the water and cover the pot. Reduce the heat to medium and simmer for 35 minutes. Remove with a slotted spoon. Makes 12 to 15 matzo balls.

For the soup: In a stockpot combine the chicken, veal bone, onions, celery, and carrots. Add the water and salt. Bring to a boil over high heat. Use a slotted spoon or strainer to remove any foam that rises to the surface of the soup. Reduce the heat to medium and simmer for 4 hours. If the liquid becomes too concentrated, add more water during the cooking time. Add the sweet potatoes, dill, and parsley. Simmer for an additional 45 minutes. Remove from the heat. Using a large, slotted spoon, remove the chicken pieces and veal bone to a bowl. Discard veal bone. When the chicken is cool enough to handle, remove the skin and bones and place the meat back into the soup. Serve the soup with matzo balls floating on top. Garnish with the parsley.

Makes 10 to 12 servings

Chicken soup is so deeply embedded in the Jewish tradition that it has become the defining dish for Jewish grandmothers. Everyone makes it slightly differently, but it always symbolizes nurturing. Matzo balls started out as a Passover garnish, as they were made from the unleavened bread served during the holiday. They now accompany chicken soup all year. Cooks are often judged by the consistency of their matzo balls—the lighter the better.

Spicy Chicken and Rice Flu Chaser Soup

This soup can't substitute for a visit to a doctor, but it should help settle your stomach, clear your sinuses, and improve your mood. (For the surprising story of how I developed the recipe, see page 56.) We go through gallons of it every winter, when people are desperate to alleviate the sniffles, coughs, and other symptoms of the viruses that make their annual rounds.

20 whole cloves garlic, peeled	1 tablespoon lemon zest
1 1/2 cups olive oil	2 teaspoons dried mint leaves
1 whole chicken, about 5 pounds	1 teaspoon ground cinnamon
1 large Spanish onion, peeled and diced	1/2 teaspoon cayenne pepper
6 carrots, peeled and sliced	2 bay leaves
3 ribs celery, diced	2 tablespoons chopped fresh basil
12 cups chicken stock, plus additional if needed	3 cups cooked white or jasmine rice
3/4 cup fresh lemon juice	Kosher salt, to taste

Preheat the oven to 375 degrees. Place the garlic cloves in a small, ovenproof casserole. Pour the olive oil over the garlic. Bake for 45 to 50 minutes, until the garlic is soft, brown, and caramelized. Strain the oil to use in other recipes. Mash the cloves and set aside.

In a stockpot place the chicken, onion, carrots, and celery. Pour the chicken stock over the chicken and bring to a boil over medium-high heat. Add the roasted garlic cloves, lemon juice, lemon zest, mint, cinnamon, cayenne pepper, and bay leaves. Reduce the heat to medium and simmer for

$2^{1}/2$ hours, or until the chicken is very tender. Remove the chicken carefully and place on a plate to cool.

Remove the soup from the heat. If it looks too thick, add 1 to 2 cups of stock or water. When the chicken is cool enough to handle, remove the skin and bones, and add the meat back to the soup. Bring to a boil over medium-high heat. Taste, adding more lemon juice if you like. Add the basil, rice, and salt. Remove the bay leaves. Stir and serve.

Makes 8 to 10 servings

Holiday Chicken Soup

This is one of the few recipes I reserve for special occasions at home because it just doesn't suit the tremendous quantities I usually make at the store. It needs to reduce and fortify all day so the broth becomes almost like a demi-glace—clear, thick, and concentrated. The vegetables that are added towards the end need to be carefully cut into small pieces. The contrast between the rich, clear broth and the delicate vegetables makes this a treat. I always serve this soup at Druker family holiday gatherings.

Broth

- 5 to 6 pounds chicken parts, preferably thighs
- 2 large veal bones
- 2 large onions, peeled and halved
- 6 ribs celery
- 2 parsnips, peeled and cut into thirds
- 5 carrots, peeled and cut into thirds
- 2 bay leaves
- 1 bunch fresh parsley
  Kosher salt, to taste
- 16 cups water

Vegetables

- 6 carrots, peeled and julienned
- 2 large scallions, trimmed and julienned
- 6 parsnips, peeled and julienned
- 1/4 cup chopped fresh parsley
- 1/4 cup chopped fresh dill
- 2 to 3 high-quality chicken bouillon cubes, such as Better Than Bouillon brand
  Kosher salt, to taste

For the broth: Combine the chicken, veal bones, onions, celery, parsnips, carrots, bay leaves, parsley, and salt in a stockpot. Pour in the water. Bring to a boil over medium-high heat. Reduce the heat to medium and simmer for 8 hours, adding more water if the liquid becomes too thick. In a colander set over a large bowl, drain the soup. Discard the solids and return the stock to the pot.

For the vegetables: Bring the stock back to a boil over medium-high heat. Add the carrots, scallions, parsnips, parsley, dill, and bouillon. Continue to boil for 10 to 15 minutes. Season with salt.

Makes 8 to 10 servings (8 ounces each)

Greek Orzo, Lemon, and Chicken Soup

This is by far one of the most requested soups from our store. Some customers actually get angry when they do not see it on the menu. What makes this Greek classic so appealing is its intensely rich chicken broth, infused with lemon juice and zest. It is also enhanced with threads of cooked eggs, vibrant leaves of fresh spinach, and orzo. The soup is definitely a spirit lifter. I always like to see the response when I ladle out a sample for someone who admits to not feeling well. A smile—and an order for an entire bowl—usually follow. I also like to make this soup during Easter because it features eggs.

10 cups homemade chicken stock

3/4 cup orzo

4 eggs, lightly beaten with a fork

Juice of 3 lemons

Zest of 2 lemons

1 cup coarsely chopped cooked chicken

1 pound fresh spinach

Kosher salt and freshly ground black pepper, to taste

In a stockpot bring the stock to a boil over high heat. Add the orzo and cook 5 minutes. While stirring constantly, drizzle in the eggs and continue stirring for at least 30 seconds, or until the eggs cook into threads.

Add the lemon juice, lemon zest, chicken, spinach, salt, and pepper. Return to a boil. Immediately remove from the heat and serve.

Makes 6 to 8 servings

Orzo is a type of pasta that looks like an overgrown grain of rice. It works well in soups because it adds starch without much bulk. It is a favorite in Italian and Greek soups, and has also made its way into Middle Eastern rice pilafs. Look for it in the pasta section of a supermarket, or at a specialty Italian or Middle Eastern market.

Under the Sea

Seafood from local waters has sustained New Englanders ever since the Pilgrims arrived. I can't imagine living anywhere that didn't have such easy access to fresh lobsters, scallops, crabs, oysters, and fish. It makes all those coastal "nor'easter" storms worth enduring. Fishing boats go out year-round, bringing back plenty of fresh ingredients to turn into classics like cioppino or bouillabaisse. Shellfish is a starting point for many New England Soup Factory recipes because it can hold its own so well against more assertive ingredients. Curry powder and ginger offset mussels in one of our bisque recipes. Another pair is crabmeat and Havarti cheese. For people who can't decide which kind of seafood they like best, we put six different kinds, including mussels and cherrystone clams, into our Lusty Fish Stew.

I caught my first fish one summer when I went away to camp in Connecticut. I was nine years old. Our counselor, Tom, taught fishing at a small dam connected to the lake. We would sit there as patiently as is possible for children until one of us finally landed one. After days of watching everyone else triumphantly reel one in, I finally felt a tug on my pole. Something was practically pulling all fifty pounds of me into the water! My grin was about as wide as the lake. When I finally pulled up the wriggling six-incher, I could not wait to take it off the hook. All I could think about was bringing it to the dining hall so that Smitty, the cook, could fry it up for us.

Tom had other ideas. He helped me pull the fish off the hook, but then he immediately threw it back into the water. I was horrified! I screamed, "What are you doing? That was my fish!" Tom told me that we were not allowed to kill the fish or any living thing at camp, including bugs and plants. (Little did he know how many mosquitoes we all swatted.) I cried the whole walk back to my bunk and would not even look at him.

That evening at dinner, I went to see Smitty. I told him that I had caught a beautiful fish for him to cook, but Tom would not let me keep it. Smitty looked at me and smiled as he said, "Don't worry, we are having fish sticks tomorrow for lunch." That made me feel a little better, but I still wanted to taste the fish I had caught. Maybe that's why I crave fresh seafood to this day.

Crab and Havarti Bisque with Dill

Crab is so succulent and sweet that you almost can't go wrong with any recipe. Cheese complements crab especially well. My friend, Ellen, makes appetizers with these two ingredients, and I devour them every time. That's what inspired this soup. Ellen's husband, Peter, also known as Mr. Fish, catches fresh crabs right off of his boat in Green Harbor on Boston's South Shore. Their fresh, briny flavor makes them a real treat. Extending the appetizer theme, this soup goes well with homemade cheddar biscuits.

3 tablespoons butter	1 pound crabmeat
3 whole cloves garlic, peeled	8 slices (1/2 pound) Havarti cheese
1 large Spanish onion, peeled and diced	3 teaspoons dry mustard
2 carrots, peeled and sliced	2 cups heavy cream
2 ribs celery, diced	6 dashes Worcestershire sauce
3 potatoes, peeled and diced into 3/4-inch cubes	6 dashes Tabasco sauce
4 tablespoons tomato paste	3 tablespoons chopped fresh dill
8 cups lobster stock	Kosher salt and freshly ground black pepper, to taste
1 cup sherry	

Melt the butter in a stockpot over medium-high heat. Add the garlic, onion, carrots, celery, and potatoes. Sauté, stirring frequently, for 10 minutes. Add the tomato paste, stock, and sherry. Bring to a boil. Reduce the heat to medium, cover the pot, and simmer for 35 to 40 minutes. Remove from the heat. Add the crabmeat, cheese, and the mustard.

Let the cheese melt into the soup. Puree the soup in the pot using a hand blender or working in batches with a regular blender until smooth. Return to the stove. Add the cream, Worcestershire sauce, Tabasco sauce, dill, salt, and pepper and stir thoroughly.

Makes 10 to 12 servings

If you aren't lucky enough to have a friend who supplies you with just-caught seafood, use fresh or frozen crab in this recipe. Avoid the canned variety, as its quality doesn't tend to be high enough for this soup.

69

Curried Mussel Bisque

I didn't start eating mussels until I was in my twenties, but I soon made up for lost time, especially during the three years that I lived on Cape Cod. What is most fun about this soup is being able to sip the saffron-colored broth out of a mussel shell instead of a spoon. Its complex flavor comes from the combination of tomatoes, white wine, and fish stock, with curry powder and ginger spicing it up. The mussels open during cooking, and the tender meat can be nudged out with a fork.

36	fresh mussels	6	cups fish stock or clam juice
3	tablespoons olive oil	1	cup white wine
3	cloves garlic, minced	2 1/2	teaspoons yellow curry powder
1	tablespoon minced fresh ginger	1	teaspoon ground coriander
1	large Spanish onion, peeled and diced		Pinch of crushed red pepper flakes
2	ribs celery, diced	2	tablespoons chopped fresh cilantro
2	carrots, peeled and diced	1	tablespoon brown sugar
2	cups (16 ounces) canned stewed tomatoes		Kosher salt and freshly ground black pepper, to taste

Fill the sink or a clean bowl with ice water. Soak the mussels for 20 minutes to remove grit from the shells. Drain the water. Using a brush scrub the shells well and remove the beards (rough, fibrous patches on the sides of the shells).

Heat a stockpot over medium-high heat. Add the olive oil, garlic, ginger, onion, celery, and carrots. Sauté for 10 minutes. Add the mussels to the pot and stir to coat with the vegetables and oil. Add the tomatoes, stock, wine, curry, coriander, and red pepper flakes. Bring to a boil. Reduce the heat to medium, cover the pot, and simmer until all of the mussel shells have opened. Add the cilantro, brown sugar, salt, and pepper, and stir gently. Serve immediately.

Makes 8 to 10 servings

This soup makes an easy, informal summer meal for friends. Ladle each serving into a big, wide bowl. Set out an empty bowl for the empty mussel shells, and plenty of extra napkins. Slices of crusty bread are great for sopping up the extra broth.

Lusty Fish Stew

photo on
page 66

If you're tempted to walk up to a seafood counter and pick out one thing from each display, try this stew. A take-off on French bouillabaisse, it combines six kinds of seafood in a tomato and saffron-enhanced broth. There's not any racy story behind its name. I was just trying to emphasize its robustness.

3   tablespoons olive oil

3   cloves garlic, minced

1   Spanish onion, diced

1/2   cup diced celery

2   large carrots, peeled and thickly cut on the bias

1   can (28 ounces) whole tomatoes

4   cups clam juice

1   cup dry white wine

3   teaspoons fennel seeds

    A few pinches Spanish saffron

1   teaspoon dried oregano

1   teaspoon dried basil

1   cup uncooked medium pasta shells

1/2   pound halibut fillet

1/2   pound salmon fillet

12   cherrystone clams

12   mussels

1/2   pound peeled and deveined shrimp

1/2   pound scallops

    Kosher salt and freshly ground black pepper, to taste

In a stockpot heat the olive oil over medium-high heat. Add the garlic, onion, celery, and carrots. Sauté for 5 minutes. Add the tomatoes, clam juice, wine, fennel seeds, saffron, oregano, and basil. Bring to a boil. Lower the heat to medium and simmer for 10 minutes. Add the pasta shells and simmer for 5 minutes. Cut the halibut and salmon into large chunks and add to the pot. Add the clams, mussels, shrimp, and scallops. Cover the pot and cook until the clam and mussel shells open, 10 to 12 minutes. Season with salt and pepper.

Makes 8 servings

Spicy Shrimp and Rice Soup

I thrive on the mouth-tingling jolt of chile peppers, curry powder, and other vivid spices. As a result, our customers know they can count on at least one spicy soup on our menu each day. Some people automatically order whatever it is. This soup starts out mildly enough with fish stock and tomatoes. Then it gets a dose of scorching Scotch bonnet chile peppers, one of the hottest in the chile pepper family. As the soup simmers, its fragrance makes me feel like I am already taking a sip. My face gets very pink, my chest opens up, and I start to giggle as if someone is tickling me. All this before I've even lifted the spoon to my mouth!

Rice

- 3 cups water
- 1 tablespoon salted butter
  Dash of salt
- 1 1/2 cups jasmine rice

Soup

- 3 tablespoons olive oil
- 5 cloves garlic, minced
- 1 large Spanish onion, peeled and diced
- 3 ribs celery, diced
- 3 carrots, peeled and diced
- 1 yellow bell pepper, diced
- 12 cups fish stock or clam juice
- 2 cups (16 ounces) canned diced tomatoes
- 1 teaspoon fennel seeds
- 2 generous pinches saffron threads
- 1 teaspoon dried oregano
- 2 pounds raw small (36-45 per pound) shrimp
- 4 cups cooked jasmine rice (from recipe)
- 1/4 cup freshly squeezed lime juice
- 5 dashes green Tabasco sauce
- 1 teaspoon (more, to taste) Scotch bonnet chile pepper, minced
  Kosher salt and freshly ground black pepper, to taste

For the rice: In a 3-quart saucepan, add the water, butter, and salt. Bring to a boil over high heat. Add the jasmine rice. Stir and bring back to a boil. Cover the pot and reduce the heat to low. Simmer for 15 to 18 minutes, or until all the water is absorbed and the rice is soft. Fluff with a fork.

For the soup: In a stockpot heat the olive oil over medium-high heat. Add the garlic, onion, celery, carrots, and yellow bell pepper. Sauté for 10 minutes. Add the stock, tomatoes, fennel seeds, saffron, and oregano. Bring to a boil. Reduce the heat to medium and simmer for 30 minutes. Add the shrimp and cook for 10 minutes more. Add the rice, lime juice, Tabasco sauce, chile pepper, salt, and pepper.

Makes 8 to 10 servings

Wear rubber gloves when you are cutting hot peppers, and wash the cutting board well afterwards, as the oils can irritate your hands. If you forget to use gloves, wash your hands thoroughly after you are done cutting, and avoid rubbing your eyes (that includes inserting or removing contact lenses) for at least an hour.

Curried Shrimp and Rice Soup with Okra

This recipe calls for a long list of ingredients, but its fragrance is worth all of the shopping and prepping. Curry powder makes the broth a golden hue, while the ginger, coriander, and cayenne pepper deepen the flavor. The shrimp absorb all of these spices, adding a burst of flavor to each bite. The addition of coconut, ginger, and okra makes it feel as though you have just traveled to some exotic spot to enjoy a steaming bowl of bliss. Each spoonful is like a mini adventure, even when you never leave your kitchen chair.

2 tablespoons olive oil

3 cloves garlic, minced

1½ cups diced onions

¼ cup diced celery

2 cups diced carrots

1½ cups diced red bell peppers

4 tablespoons minced fresh ginger

2 tablespoons curry powder

2 teaspoons ground coriander

½ teaspoon cayenne pepper

1 cup shredded coconut

2 cups (16 ounces) canned diced tomatoes, drained

12 cups fish stock or clam juice

2 pounds large raw shrimp, peeled and deveined

1 can (16 ounces) coconut milk

3 tablespoons honey

3 cups cooked white rice

1 pound sliced fresh or frozen okra

1 bunch fresh cilantro, chopped

2 tablespoons freshly squeezed lime juice

Kosher salt, to taste

Heat a stockpot over medium-high heat and add the olive oil. Add the garlic, onions, celery, carrots, red peppers, and ginger. Sauté for 5 minutes. Add the curry powder, coriander, and cayenne pepper. Stir well. Add the shredded coconut, tomatoes, and stock. Bring to a boil. Reduce the heat to medium.

Cover the pot and simmer for 20 minutes. Add the shrimp. Cover the pot again and simmer for 10 minutes more. Add the coconut milk, honey, rice, okra, cilantro, lime juice, and salt. Cook for 5 to 7 minutes.

Makes 10 to 12 servings

Crab Gumbo

Crab gumbo is somewhat of a novelty in chowder-crazed New England. That is exactly why I make it. I like giving people a sample of food from other places. A specialty in Louisiana, gumbo combines influences from the French, Spanish, and Africans who settled the area. Recipes vary, but usually contain okra and a combination of meats and seafood. Crabmeat, okra, rice, and filé powder (made from ground sassafras leaves) give the soup its body. Every bite contains a jazzy mix of vegetables, seafood, and spices.

Roux

- 6 tablespoons butter
- 1 cup flour

Gumbo

- 2 tablespoons olive oil
- 4 cloves garlic, minced
- 1 large Spanish onion, peeled and diced
- 2 ribs celery, diced
- 4 carrots, peeled and sliced
- 1 can (28 ounces) whole tomatoes, broken into pieces with kitchen scissors or the back of a spoon
- 8 cups lobster or fish stock
- 2 cups tomato juice
- 2 teaspoons ground coriander
- 2 bay leaves
- Roux (from recipe)
- 1 cup white wine
- 1 pound crabmeat, broken into pieces
- 1 cup corn kernels, fresh or frozen
- 2 cups fresh okra, sliced into 3/4-inch long pieces
- 1 tablespoon filé powder (available at specialty spice shops)
- 1/4 teaspoon cayenne pepper
- 8 dashes Tabasco sauce
- 4 dashes Worcestershire sauce
- 1 1/2 cups cooked white rice
- Kosher salt and freshly ground black pepper, to taste

For the roux: Preheat the oven to 350 degrees. In an ovenproof sauté pan melt the butter. Add the flour and stir, moving it around until it no longer sticks to the sides of the pan. Transfer the pan to the oven and bake for 20 minutes, or until lightly golden. Watch carefully so it does not burn. Remove from the oven and set aside.

For the soup: Heat a stockpot over medium-high heat. Add the olive oil, garlic, onion, celery, and carrots. Sauté for 7 minutes. Add the tomatoes, stock, tomato juice, coriander, and bay leaves. Bring to a boil. Reduce the heat to medium. Cover the pot and simmer for 10 minutes. Using a hand blender or a regular blender, blend the roux with the white wine until liquefied and there are no lumps. Add the roux-wine mixture, crabmeat, corn, okra, filé powder, cayenne pepper, Tabasco sauce, and Worcestershire sauce to the soup pot. Simmer over medium-high heat, stirring frequently, for 30 minutes. Add the cooked rice and season with salt and pepper. Remove the bay leaves before serving.

Makes 12 servings

The velvety texture in the base of this gumbo depends on roux, a paste of butter and flour that has been cooked together. At the New England Soup Factory, we start the roux on the stovetop and then transfer it to the oven, where it bakes until it becomes a pale, golden color. At that point, it has developed a lovely, very rich, toasted flavor. The roux simultaneously thickens and flavors the lobster or fish stock.

Championship Chowders

Nowhere in the United States is chowder more popular than in New England. Clam chowder (the creamy, white kind, made without tomatoes) has become the most identifiable chowder, but there are many varieties. What all chowders have in common is their thick, chunky consistency. The word is thought to come from the French chaudière, a special kind of cauldron. At the New England Soup Factory, classic New England clam chowder is a top seller, but that's only the beginning of our chowder menu. Corn makes a great chowder base, especially when combined with sweet potatoes, or bacon and cheddar cheese. So does pumpkin. When we have a lot of different varieties on the menu at once, it's like having our own chowder cook-off in the store.

When my husband, Paul, and I had just graduated from culinary school, we ran a restaurant on Cape Cod. A man in the neighborhood where Paul had grown up had just purchased the restaurant and recruited Paul to manage it. He agreed, but only if we could work as a team. This old-style tavern badly needed some TLC. It was musty and dusty, and the menu hadn't changed in decades. We spent the first few days scrubbing the floors, polishing the brass, and hiring waitresses (I somehow ended up being the token brunette). When it came time to plan the menu, we added lots of exciting and imaginative dishes, but there was one thing we could never change. We had to keep New England clam chowder on the menu. Every restaurant on the Cape—except for Chinese places—serves chowder.

I was too young and inexperienced to be the head chef, so Paul hired a chef from Hyannis named Ron Prouty. Ron was a real pro, and he could make anything. He taught me his techniques for all the traditional foods on Cape Cod, including chowder. I would make batch after batch, but I never developed enough confidence. I kept questioning him every time. "How do you chop the salt pork?" I would ask. "How much celery salt?" Ron would patiently listen, and then reply, "Marj, that's all I am going to tell you." I realized that I just needed to watch him for awhile. After that, and after experimenting with many more batches, I finally got the recipe right. I really credit Ron for teaching me to make chowder just like a native Cape Codder.

New England Clam Chowder

photo on
page 78

New England clam chowder can be found on almost every menu from Connecticut to Maine. It is even sold at Boston Red Sox games at Fenway Park. Locally-caught clams, chunks of white potatoes, and cream are just a few of the ingredients that give this dish its personality. The chowder is one of our most popular soups, as it's true New England soul food. It warms you up all winter, but I also think it's a perfect summer treat. Take a thermos to the beach, wait for the sun to go down, then pour it into mugs. The little bit of sand that sneaks onto your spoon only enhances the texture.

3 tablespoons butter
1 Spanish onion, peeled and diced
3 ribs celery, diced
2 small pieces (about 2 ounces each) salt pork
5 potatoes, peeled and cut into 3/4-inch cubes
5 cups clam juice
2 bay leaves

1 teaspoon dried tarragon
1 teaspoon celery salt
1 1/2 pounds minced clams, preferably fresh
5 dashes Worcestershire sauce
2 cups heavy cream
Kosher salt and freshly ground black pepper, to taste
Oyster crackers, for serving

In a stockpot melt the butter over medium-high heat. Add the onion, celery, and salt pork. Sauté for 5 to 7 minutes. Add the potatoes, clam juice, bay leaves, tarragon, and celery salt. Bring to a boil. Reduce the heat to medium, cover the pot, and simmer for 35 minutes. Add the clams and simmer, uncovered, for 5 minutes. Add the Worcestershire sauce, cream, salt, and pepper. Simmer an additional 7 minutes and remove from the heat. Remove the bay leaves. Garnish with oyster crackers or common crackers and a sprinkle of celery salt.

Makes 10 to 12 servings

Common crackers used to be a favorite chowder garnish in New England. They look like giant oyster crackers, with a crisp exterior, and a hollow middle. They can be split and spread with butter or cheddar cheese. These crackers have become somewhat quaint, and are now available mostly at specialty stores. Oyster crackers have replaced them as the chowder garnish of choice.

Boston Fish Chowder

New Englanders have been making fish chowder ever since the 1700s, though the recipe has evolved over time. Some early versions called for red wine or ketchup before preferences changed to a creamy, white combination of fish, potatoes, salt pork, and seasonings. My version doesn't stray far from tradition. I like to use haddock, but you can use any other white fish (such as cod or mackerel), as long as it has a bit of firmness to it. Fish chowder is a rather rustic soup. It is best served in large mugs with plenty of salty oyster crackers on top. I especially like it on a cool, rainy day.

3 tablespoons butter	2 bay leaves
1 large Spanish onion, peeled and diced	2 1/2 pounds haddock, cut into bite-size pieces
2 ribs celery, diced	2 cups heavy cream
2 small pieces (about 2 ounces each) salt pork	Kosher salt and freshly ground black pepper, to taste
4 cups red new potatoes, peeled and diced into 3/4-inch cubes	2 tablespoons chopped fresh parsley
6 cups fish stock or clam juice	Oyster crackers, for serving
1 teaspoon dried thyme	

In a stockpot melt the butter over medium-high heat. Add the onion, celery, and salt pork. Sauté for 10 minutes or until the onion turn a light golden color. Add the potatoes and sauté for 3 minutes more. Add the stock, thyme, and bay leaves. Bring to a boil. Reduce the heat to medium and simmer until the potatoes are just tender, about 20 minutes.

Add the haddock and gently stir for 5 minutes. Add the heavy cream and season with salt and pepper. Stir in the parsley. Remove the salt pork, if desired, or leave in for more flavor. Remove the bay leaves. Serve with plenty of oyster crackers.

Makes 6 to 8 servings

Manhattan Clam Chowder

photo on page 78 (top)

What I like most about Manhattan clam chowder is its zesty broth, loaded with bits of chewy clams. I like to make my version spicy and serve it with a side of garlic bread. Rhode Islanders serve a similar dish called Rhode Island red chowder. It is basically the same chowder as Manhattan with a different name.

3 tablespoons olive oil	2 bay leaves
3 cloves garlic, minced	2 pinches saffron threads
1 Spanish onion, peeled and diced	2 teaspoons dried oregano
2 ribs celery, diced	2 teaspoons dried basil
1 red bell pepper, seeded and diced	1 teaspoon crushed red pepper flakes
4 large Yukon Gold potatoes, peeled and cut into 3/4-inch cubes	2 cups chopped clams, preferably fresh
4 cups (32 ounces) canned stewed tomatoes	5 dashes Worcestershire sauce
8 cups clam juice	Kosher salt and freshly ground black pepper, to taste

Heat a stockpot over medium-high heat. Add the olive oil, garlic, onion, celery, and bell pepper. Sauté for 8 minutes. Add the potatoes, tomatoes, clam juice, bay leaves, saffron, oregano, basil, and crushed red pepper flakes. Bring to a boil. Reduce the heat to medium and simmer until the potatoes are tender, about 35 minutes. Add the chopped clams, Worcestershire sauce, salt, and pepper. Simmer an additional 5 minutes. Remove the bay leaves before serving.

Makes 6 to 8 servings

The longstanding rivalry between Boston and New York extends to chowder as well as baseball. Bostonians swear that chowder made with tomatoes shouldn't be called chowder. (Eleanor Early, author of the New England Sampler, once declared, "Tomatoes and clams have no more affinity than ice cream and horseradish.") New Yorkers think it's the best kind. There are plenty of native New Yorkers in Boston who still get a craving for their Manhattan clam chowder. I try to satisfy them, though I try not to serve it when the arch-rival New York Yankees are in town!

Corn and Roasted Red Pepper Chowder

Sometimes customers ask me if I ever make just plain corn chowder and I frankly tell them I never do anything plain. This chowder is a perfect example of that. I feel like I have been making it forever, because it was one of my specialties long before I opened the New England Soup Factory. Chris, one of our managers, loves this soup and I try to make it for him often. It's like a reward for a job well done. The pureed roasted red peppers gives the soup a glorious glow and taste.

6 tablespoons salted butter	3 pounds frozen or fresh corn kernels
2 cups diced onions	2 cans (16 ounces each) creamed corn
1/2 cup diced celery	2 tablespoons cornstarch dissolved in 4 tablespoons cold water
1 cup diced carrots	2 cups light cream
3 cloves garlic, minced	2 cups roasted red peppers, pureed until smooth
4 to 5 Yukon gold potatoes, peeled and cut into 1/2-inch cubes	1/4 cup chopped fresh cilantro
6 cups chicken stock or broth	2 teaspoons Tabasco sauce
2 teaspoons ground coriander	Kosher salt and freshly ground black pepper, to taste
1 teaspoon ground bay leaves	

■ In a stockpot melt the butter over medium-high heat. Add the onions, celery, carrots, and garlic. Sauté for 5 to 7 minutes. Add the potatoes and sauté for 5 minutes more. Add the broth and bring to a boil. Reduce the heat to medium and simmer until the potatoes soften but don't lose their shape, about 10 minutes. Add the coriander, bay leaves, and corn. Bring back to a boil and cook for 5 minutes. Add the creamed corn and the cornstarch-water mixture. Return to a boil and cook for 1 to 2 minutes. Add the cream, red peppers, cilantro, Tabasco sauce, salt, and pepper. Bring the soup to a slow simmer for 2 minutes.

Makes 10 to 12 servings

In this recipe, it makes little difference if you substitute frozen corn kernels for fresh ones. The chowder tastes great either way. If you are using fresh corn, one ear yields about 1/2 cup of kernels.

Cheddar-Corn Chowder with Bacon and Scallions

Our customers go wild for this tasty combination of crisp bits of bacon, sharp cheddar cheese, and crunchy scallions. These flavors work so well together, you almost can't go wrong when you put them in a soup. People sometimes order a dozen bowls at a time—one for everyone at work. It makes me so happy to think that one whole office is slurping up this chowder for lunch.

1   pound uncooked bacon, diced

1   large Spanish onion, peeled and diced

3   carrots, peeled and diced

2   ribs celery, diced

3   cloves garlic, minced

5   medium red bliss potatoes, diced into 3/4-inch cubes

6   cups chicken stock

1/4   teaspoon cayenne pepper

2   teaspoons ground coriander

2   cans (each 16 ounces) whole kernel corn, drained

2   cans (each 16 ounces) creamed corn

1   pound (16 ounces) sharp cheddar cheese, grated

2   cups heavy cream

4   dashes Worcestershire sauce

    Kosher salt and freshly ground black pepper, to taste

2   bunches scallions, sliced

■ Heat a stockpot over medium-high heat and add the bacon. Cook the bacon until brown and crispy. Remove the bacon from the pot and set aside on paper towels to drain. Discard all but 2 tablespoons of the bacon drippings. Add the onion, carrots, celery, and garlic to the drippings and sauté for 5 minutes. Add the potatoes, stock, cayenne pepper, and coriander. Bring to a boil. Reduce the heat to medium and simmer for 35 minutes. Add the whole kernel corn, creamed corn, cheese, and cream. Simmer an additional 7 minutes. Season with the Worcestershire sauce, salt, and pepper. Stir in the scallions and crispy bacon pieces.

Makes 10 to 12 servings

Sweet Potato and Corn Chowder

If you think chowder is defined by clams, you haven't tasted this version. It is a treasure chest of flavors and textures: Chunks of sweet potato, kernels of corn, pureed vegetables, and the surprise seasoning of coriander. Each bite can give you a different combination. At the New England Soup Factory, it is a fall favorite that has been brought home for many a Thanksgiving dinner.

7 large sweet potatoes, peeled, divided	1/4 cup packed brown sugar
4 tablespoons butter	1 tablespoon ground coriander
2 cloves garlic, chopped	2 cups heavy cream
1 Spanish onion, peeled and diced	1 can (16 ounces) whole kernel corn, drained
2 ribs celery, diced	1 can (16 ounces) can creamed corn
3 carrots, peeled and diced	Kosher salt and freshly ground black pepper, to taste
8 cups chicken stock	
5 dashes Worcestershire sauce	

■ In a 3-quart saucepan bring 1 1/2 quarts of salted water to a boil over high heat. Dice 2 of the sweet potatoes and add to the boiling water. Boil for 10 minutes. Drain in a colander. Rinse with cool water and set aside. Roughly chop the remaining 5 sweet potatoes.

■ In a stockpot melt the butter over medium-high heat. Add the garlic, onion, celery, carrots, and the 5 chopped sweet potatoes. Sauté for 10 minutes. Add the stock and bring to a boil. Reduce the heat to medium and simmer until the sweet potatoes are soft and tender, 30 to 35 minutes. Remove from the heat and add the Worcestershire sauce, brown sugar, coriander, and cream. Puree the soup in the pot using a hand blender or working in batches with a regular blender until smooth and creamy. Add the reserved sweet potatoes, whole kernel corn, and creamed corn. Return the soup to the stove and simmer an additional 5 to 7 minutes. Season with salt and pepper.

Makes 10 to 12 servings

Pumpkin-Shrimp Chowder

Our customers are always game for a new and interesting variety of chowder. This one is thick and hearty, filled with chunks of pumpkin, shrimp, and cubes of potatoes. The unusual taste comes from the pumpkin base and seafood stock. Putting these two ingredients together is kind of like a mixed marriage between sweet pumpkin and astringent stock, but it works. It gives you a new way to prepare pumpkin instead of pie.

1 1/2 Spanish onions, peeled and diced, divided

4 ribs celery, sliced, divided

2 pounds pumpkin or butternut squash, peeled and cut into chunks, divided

2 tablespoons olive oil

3 tablespoons butter

3 cloves garlic, minced

4 carrots, peeled and sliced

1 can (16 ounces) pumpkin puree

6 cups lobster or fish stock

1 cup sherry

2 teaspoons ground coriander

1 teaspoon celery salt

1/2 cup packed brown sugar

1 pound small raw shrimp, peeled and deveined

2 cups heavy cream

2 cups diced, cooked white potatoes

1/2 bunch fresh basil, chopped (about 1/4 cup)

5 dashes Worcestershire sauce

4 dashes Tabasco sauce

Kosher salt and freshly ground black pepper, to taste

Common crackers or oyster crackers, for serving

■ Set aside 3/4 cup onion, 2 ribs celery, and 11/2 cups pumpkin. In a sauté pan heat the olive oil over medium-high heat. Add the remaining onion, celery, and pumpkin. Sauté until soft and golden, 12 to 15 minutes. Remove from the heat and set aside.

■ In a stockpot melt the butter. Add the reserved onion and celery, the garlic, and carrots. Sauté for 5 minutes. Add the reserved pumpkin and sauté 5 minutes more. Add the pumpkin puree, stock, sherry, coriander, and celery salt. Bring to a boil. Reduce the heat to medium, cover the pot, and simmer until the pumpkin is soft and tender, about 35 minutes. Add the brown sugar. Puree the soup in the pot using a hand blender or working in batches with a regular blender until smooth. Return the soup to the heat and add the shrimp. Return to a simmer for 4 to 5 minutes, or until the shrimp are cooked through. Add the cream, potatoes, basil, Worcestershire sauce, Tabasco sauce, salt, pepper, and the sautéed vegetables. Stir well. Serve with common or oyster crackers.

Makes 12 servings

Any kind of pumpkin—even a misshapen one—will do when you're carving a jack-o-lantern. For cooking, you get the best results from a sugar pumpkin, which is sweeter and less stringy than a regular field pumpkin. It's hard to distinguish a sugar pumpkin from its cousins, so ask for help if the pumpkins at the market are not labeled.

Old-World Flavors

These time-honored recipes prove why they have nourished people for generations. Some come from the Jewish traditions that were part of my childhood. Others recreate classics such as pasta fagioli from Italy, mulligatawny soup from India, and hot and sour soup from China. New England Soup Factory customers always appreciate the chance to order something familiar, though in a few cases I have used traditional flavors as a starting point for my own inventions.

My daughter, Emily, was just three years old when my husband and I opened the New England Soup Factory. She attended a wonderful day care center where the teachers were loving and gentle. Many came from Russia and were not afraid to take the children out to play even if it was twenty-six degrees outside. When I picked up Emily at 5:00 p.m. each day, she was never ready to leave. She felt completely at home there.

I always packed a dinner for Emily and me before I left the Soup Factory because I was too tired to cook when I got home, and Daddy was still at work. All I could get her to eat was chicken noodle soup with a matzo ball. She simply was not ready yet for clam chowder, minestrone, and all of the other sophisticated flavors I had to offer. Then again, it was no problem getting her to eat dessert from the Soup Factory. She would always devour the brownie I brought home because she loves chocolate.

After a year of this routine, I picked up Emily one day and noticed that she was in a bad mood. I strapped her into her car seat and headed home, figuring I'd help cheer her up after we arrived. Then, from the back seat, Emily angrily called out, "Mom, what's for dinner? Soup and brownies?" Startled, I looked at her in the rearview mirror. Then I started to laugh uncontrollably. I guess she was finally tired of the same dinner every night for a year—and who could blame her? It was then that I realized it was important for me to do more than bring home the food I had made at work. I can't say that we have a gourmet meal every night, but now I do make the time to cook for my family—and vary the menu!

Lima Bean and Barley Soup

When I was a child, I used to love to slurp this soup when I ate at a Jewish delicatessen. I would always order a bowl—never a measly cup—and eat it with all of the free pickles I could get the waitress to bring. My mother would scold, "Marjorie, you are going to make yourself sick eating all of those things!" Yet somehow, I always knew my stomach could handle this meal. Now I make my own recipe with big, fat, creamy lima beans floating among chewy pearls of barley. Presoaking the lima beans in boiling water is an essential step in softening their wrinkled, tough texture.

1   pound dried large lima beans

3   tablespoons olive oil

1   large Spanish onion, peeled and diced

2   cloves garlic, minced

4   carrots, peeled and sliced into disks

3   ribs celery, diced

1/2   pound pearl barley

12   cups chicken stock, plus additional as needed

2   bay leaves

1/2   cup chopped fresh parsley

6   dashes Worcestershire sauce

1   tablespoon balsamic vinegar

Kosher salt and freshly ground black pepper, to taste

■ Combine the lima beans and 2 quarts of water in a 4- to 6-quart saucepan over high heat. Cover, bring to a boil, then turn off the heat. Let the beans sit for an hour or two. Drain before adding to the soup. In a stockpot heat the olive oil over medium-high heat. Add the onion, garlic, carrots, and celery. Sauté for 10 minutes. Add the lima beans and barley. Sauté for an additional 2 minutes. Add the stock and bay leaves. Bring to a boil. Reduce the heat to medium and simmer for 1 to 1 1/4 hours, or until the lima beans are thoroughly cooked, adding more stock if the soup looks dry. Add the parsley, Worcestershire sauce, vinegar, salt, and pepper. Remove the bay leaves before serving.

Makes 12 servings

Sweet and Sour Cabbage Soup with Dill

As old-fashioned as it sounds, this soup is one of my favorites. I think of it as Jewish soul food. Brown sugar, raisins, and maple syrup help mellow the sharpness of the cabbage. The flavor seems to carry with it the grandmotherly wisdom that life is sometimes sweet and sometimes sour, but the combination balances out. This soup is especially popular among our senior customers, who remember when their mothers made it for them back in the Old Country.

2   tablespoons canola oil

2   cups diced onions

2   cups sliced carrots

1/2 cup diced celery

1   head cabbage, diced or sliced

3/4 cup golden raisins

3 1/2 quarts chicken or beef stock

2   cups (16 ounces) canned stewed tomatoes

2   cups V-8 juice

2   cups packed brown sugar

1/2 cup maple syrup

1/2 to 3/4 cup lemon juice

1   tablespoon caraway seeds

1/4 cup chopped fresh dill

Kosher salt, to taste

■ Heat a stockpot for 2 minutes over medium-high heat. Add the canola oil, onions, carrots, and celery. Sauté for 5 minutes. Add the cabbage and sauté an additional 5 minutes. Add the raisins, stock, tomatoes, V-8 juice, brown sugar, maple syrup, lemon juice, and caraway seeds. Bring to a boil. Reduce the heat to medium and simmer for 1 1/2 hours. Remove from the heat. Add the dill and salt. Adjust the seasonings, adding more lemon juice or brown sugar, if necessary.

Makes 10 to 12 servings

Pasta Fagioli Soup with Ditalini

I was introduced to pasta fagioli when I was in my early 20s and living on Cape Cod. I worked at a small, family-run Italian gourmet shop. It was my first insight into great Italian cooking. We made everything from scratch every day. I learned how to prepare all of these new and interesting foods that I had not grown up eating. The first time I tasted pasta fagioli—an Italian soup made with macaroni, beans, and pork—I knew that my dad would love it because it contains all of his favorite flavors. It practically defines hearty and satisfying. Customers sometimes come in and tell me that my version tastes so much like their grandmother's that I must be Italian. I always think of that as the ultimate compliment.

Pork

1   (4 pound) smoked shoulder of pork
    Water, as needed

Soup

1   pound dried white navy beans
3   tablespoons olive oil
1   large Spanish onion, peeled and diced
2   ribs celery, sliced
6   carrots, peeled and sliced
4   cloves garlic, minced
3   cups (24 ounces) canned stewed tomatoes
16 cups stock (pork liquid from recipe supplemented with chicken stock), plus additional as needed

3   cups white wine
    Reserved pork meat (from recipe)
2   bay leaves
2   teaspoons dried oregano
1   tablespoon balsamic vinegar
1/2 pound fresh spinach leaves
1   cup dried ditalini pasta, cooked according to the package directions
2   tablespoons extra-virgin olive oil
1/2 cup freshly grated Parmesan cheese
1/4 cup chopped fresh parsley
    Kosher salt and freshly ground black pepper, to taste

■ For the pork: Place the pork shoulder in a stockpot. Fill the pot three-quarters of the way with water. Place on the stove and bring to a boil over high heat. Reduce the heat to medium or medium-high, cover the pot, and simmer at a rolling boil for 3 1/2 hours. Remove from the heat. Using a large fork (such as one used for grilling), carefully remove the pork from the pot. Reserve the cooking liquid. When the pork is cool enough to handle, remove all of the meat from the shoulder. Save the bone for another use. Cut the meat into bite-size pieces and set aside.

■ For the soup: Place the beans in a large, deep bowl. Add enough water to cover by 2 inches. Place in the refrigerator and soak overnight. Drain before using.

■ Heat a stockpot over medium-high heat. Add the olive oil, onion, celery, carrots, and garlic. Sauté for 8 minutes, stirring frequently. Add the soaked beans, tomatoes, stock, wine, pork, bay leaves, and oregano. Bring to a boil. Reduce the heat to medium, cover the pot, and simmer until the beans are cooked and tender, about 1 1/2 hours, adding up to 5 cups more stock or water if the liquid reduces too much. Discard the bay leaves. Remove 4 cups of the soup, puree in a blender, and return to the soup. Add the vinegar and the spinach. Toss the cooked pasta with the olive oil, cheese, and parsley. Add to the soup. Season with salt and pepper.

Makes 10 to 12 servings

In this recipe, I use ditalini, a shorter and more delicate type of macaroni than the more familiar elbows. A larger pasta shape would absorb too much of the liquid in the soup and become mushy.

Tuscan Ribollita Soup

I always crave this country-style Italian soup when I am feeling really hungry. It's comforting and filling, as the garlic bread soaks in broth with white beans and escarole. Canned beans just won't work in this recipe, as the beans need to soak overnight so they cook up plump and creamy. Toasted chunks of garlic bread give each serving a magnificently thick texture. Day-old bread works, too. I like to drizzle a bit of extra virgin olive oil on top right before serving.

Garlic Bread

- 1 baguette with a good crust
- 4 tablespoons butter, softened
- 2 cloves garlic, minced
- 1/2 teaspoon dried oregano
- 1/2 teaspoon dried basil

Soup

- 1 pound dried white beans
- 2 tablespoons olive oil
- 1 large Spanish onion, peeled and finely diced
- 3 ribs celery, finely diced

- 4 cloves garlic, minced
- 14 cups chicken stock, divided
- 1/4 cup julienned fresh basil
- 1 large head escarole, washed well and sliced into thick ribbons
- 1 tablespoon balsamic vinegar
- 1/2 teaspoon crushed red pepper flakes
- Kosher salt and freshly ground black pepper, to taste
- 1 loaf garlic bread (from recipe), torn into bite-size pieces
- Extra-virgin olive oil, for garnish

■ For the garlic bread: Preheat the oven to 375 degrees. Slice the baguette in half lengthwise. Place on a baking sheet, cut sides facing up. In a small bowl mix the butter with the garlic, oregano, and basil. Spread the butter on top of each cut side. Bake until crisp and light brown, 10 to 12 minutes.

■ For the soup: Place the beans in a deep bowl and add water to cover by 2 inches. Place in the refrigerator and soak overnight. Drain before using.

■ In a stockpot heat the olive oil over medium-high heat. Add the onion, celery, and garlic.

Sauté for 15 minutes, stirring frequently. Add the beans and sauté for an additional 2 minutes. Add 12 cups of the chicken stock. Bring to a boil. Reduce the heat to medium, cover the pot, and simmer 1 1/4 hours, or until the beans are tender. Remove from the heat. With a large spoon stir in the basil, escarole, vinegar, red pepper flakes, salt, and pepper. Add the pieces of garlic bread and stir into the soup. Return to medium-high heat. Stir well and add the remaining 2 cups chicken stock. Simmer for 10 minutes. Ladle into bowls and drizzle each with extra-virgin olive oil.

Makes 10 to 12 servings

Get a head start on your dinner by making two garlic breads—one to put in the soup, and one to serve on the side. For extra flavor sprinkle some freshly grated Parmesan cheese on top of the bread you serve on the side.

Mediterranean Chickpea, Lentil, and Rice Soup with Basil

I like to use dried chickpeas instead of canned for this particular recipe because they create a richer base for the soup.

1 pound dried chickpeas	1 teaspoon dried marjoram
4 tablespoons olive oil	2 bay leaves
1 Spanish onion, peeled and diced small	1/3 cup dried lentils
3 ribs celery, sliced	1/3 cup basmati rice
3 carrots, peeled and sliced into disks	1 tablespoon balsamic vinegar
3 cloves garlic, minced	1/4 cup chopped fresh basil
12 cups chicken or vegetable stock, plus additional as needed	Kosher salt and freshly ground black pepper, to taste
1 can (20 ounces) diced tomatoes	2 tablespoons green, fruity extra-virgin olive oil
2 cups tomato juice	

■ Place the chickpeas in a deep bowl and add water to cover by 2 inches. Place in the refrigerator to soak overnight. Drain before using.

■ In a large stockpot heat the olive oil over medium-high heat. Add the onion, celery, carrots, and garlic. Sauté for 10 minutes. Add the chickpeas, stock, tomatoes, tomato juice, marjoram, and bay leaves. Bring to a boil.

Reduce the heat to medium, cover the pot, and simmer for 1 1/4 hours. Add the lentils and rice. Simmer, covered, for an additional 35 minutes, adding 2 to 3 additional cups of water or stock if the liquid has reduced too much. Remove and discard the bay leaves. Season with the vinegar, basil, salt, pepper, and olive oil. Stir well before serving.

Makes 10 to 12 servings

Vegetarian Mulligatawny Soup

Mulligatawny originated in India, where its name comes from the word for "pepper water." That gives you a clue that the base is hot. The other key ingredient is lentils, which soak up all the other spices, giving the soup a tremendous depth of flavor. It's interesting to see how many customers order this soup without really knowing much about it. What they do remember is the "Seinfeld" television episode about the "Soup Nazi," who made delicious soup but intimidated his customers. When it first aired, mulligatawny (pronounced muhl-i-guh-taw-nee) became a really fashionable soup. It was amazing to see the effect of it at our business. Everyone came in talking about "Seinfeld" and asking for mulligatawny. We gladly served the soup, but drew the line at imitating the shop owner who yelled at everyone.

3	tablespoons olive oil	3	teaspoons yellow curry powder
4	cloves garlic, minced	3	teaspoons ground cumin
1	large Spanish onion, peeled and diced	2	teaspoons ground coriander
2	ribs celery, diced	1/2	teaspoon cayenne pepper
4	carrots, peeled and sliced	1	can (16 ounces) coconut milk
1	pound dried lentils	2	tablespoons honey
2	cups (16 ounces) canned whole tomatoes, cut into pieces	11/2	cups cooked basmati rice
1	can (16 ounces) chickpeas, rinsed and drained	1/2	bunch fresh cilantro, chopped
8	cups vegetable stock		Kosher salt and freshly ground black pepper, to taste
2	cups tomato juice		

■ Heat a stockpot over medium-high heat. Add the oil, garlic, onion, celery, and carrots. Sauté for 7 minutes. Add the lentils, tomatoes, chickpeas, stock, tomato juice, curry powder, cumin, coriander, and cayenne pepper. Bring to a boil.

Reduce the heat to medium, cover the pot, and simmer for 40 to 45 minutes. Stir in the coconut milk, honey, rice, cilantro, salt, and pepper.

Makes 12 servings

Chinese Hot and Sour Soup

The first time I ever tried hot and sour soup, I was twelve years old. My sister, Janie, and I walked from our house to our favorite local Chinese restaurant, Seven Star Mandarin, for lunch. Janie, fourteen, was in charge of ordering. She told me that we were getting this crazy-looking soup and to just eat it instead of asking a million questions about it. "You'll love it," she insisted. The soup was like nothing I had ever tasted and it was even better than Janie had predicted. Ever since then, I've been hooked on this Chinese combination of opposing flavors and textures—hot pepper, tangy vinegar, crunchy lily buds, velvety eggs.

8 cups chicken stock or broth	2 tablespoons red chile paste, such as Sriracha sauce
1/4 cup dried wood ear mushrooms	1 cup diced firm tofu
1/2 cup dried lily buds	1 cup julienned bamboo shoots
1 1/2 cups sliced shiitake mushrooms	1 bunch scallions, thinly sliced
2 large eggs, lightly beaten	2 tablespoons toasted sesame oil
6 tablespoons balsamic vinegar	4 tablespoons cornstarch dissolved in 4 tablespoons cold water
1/4 cup dark soy sauce	

■ In a stockpot combine the chicken stock and wood ear mushrooms. Bring to a boil over high heat. Add the lily buds and shiitake mushrooms. Reduce the heat to medium and simmer for 5 minutes.

■ While the mixture is still simmering whisk in the beaten eggs until cooked into threads.

Add the vinegar, soy sauce, chile sauce, tofu, bamboo shoots, scallions, sesame oil, and cornstarch-water mixture. Return to a boil. Cook for 1 minute and remove from the stove.

Makes 8 servings

The Boston area is home to many supermarket-style Asian markets in Chinatown as well as in some of the outlying neighborhoods. When I have time, I visit them to shop for the ingredients for this soup, including wood ear mushrooms, lily buds, and chile paste. I always come away with something new to try—and maybe to put into one of my soups. If you don't have an Asian market nearby, use a mail-order source.

Indonesian Carrot Soup

I was making carrot and ginger soup one morning when I felt the urge to go beyond my standard recipe. I craved something that had the flavor of a faraway place. That's when I took out my yellow curry powder, coconut milk, and other ingredients that evoked Indonesia, and got to work. The result was an intensely spicy yet sweet, golden-hued puree. One afternoon, when I was able to sneak away to have my hair done, a woman who worked at the salon came running over to me. She told me that she had eaten the Indonesian carrot soup earlier in the day, and couldn't get over how much she liked its spiciness. Later, she planned to go back for more to bring home to her vegetarian daughter. I always get so excited when customers tell me how my soup brought them such happiness. It makes all those long hours of stirring the kettles worthwhile.

3 tablespoons olive oil	1 teaspoon ground cumin
4 whole cloves garlic, peeled	1/2 teaspoon crushed red pepper flakes
1 tablespoon minced fresh ginger	8 cups vegetable stock
1 large Spanish onion, peeled and diced	1/2 cup sherry
2 ribs celery, sliced	1/2 cup honey, plus more to taste
3 pounds carrots, peeled and sliced	2 cans (16 ounces each) coconut milk
2 teaspoons ground yellow curry powder	3 tablespoons chopped fresh cilantro
2 teaspoons ground coriander	Kosher salt and freshly ground black pepper, to taste

■ Heat a stockpot over medium-high heat. Add the olive oil, garlic, ginger, onion, celery, and carrots. Sauté for 10 minutes. Add the curry, coriander, cumin, red pepper flakes, stock, and sherry. Bring to a boil. Reduce the heat to medium and simmer for 35 minutes. Remove from the heat and add the honey, coconut milk, cilantro, salt, and pepper. Puree the soup in the pot using a hand blender or working in batches with a regular blender until smooth. Add more honey if you like a sweeter soup.

Makes 10 to 12 servings

Syrian Chickpea Soup with Lemon and Tahini

photo on page 90

There are many incredible little shops near my home where I can buy all kinds of Middle Eastern foods. It's always a treat to browse the aisles of five-gallon buckets filled with every olive and pickle combination imaginable. On the shelves sit rows of brightly-colored spices and specialties like pomegranate syrup and rose petal jam. The bakery area displays fresh pita breads and sheet pans of honey-glazed baklava dusted with ground pistachios. Everything looks so irresistible that I end up staggering out the door with at least a dozen grocery bags. These shopping expeditions are what inspired me to combine Middle Eastern ingredients in a soup. The tahini from one of these stores is worth the splurge, as the flavor is incomparable. The fresh lemon and concentrated sesame of the tahini complement the nubby chickpeas.

Homemade toasted pita chips go well with this soup. Though crispy pita chips have recently become a packaged snack food phenomenon, I still think it's worth the effort to bake your own. This recipe turns out chips that taste crunchy, salty, and garlicky all at the same time—even when made from day-old pita bread. They are simple to prepare, and take just minutes to bake. I always have to hide them from Paul because he will eat them all before I can serve them. The chips and soup both go well with the Israeli chopped salad (see page 217), and make great dipping crackers for hummus.

Homemade Toasted Pita Chips

8 whole pita bread rounds

2/3 cup extra-virgin olive oil

3 teaspoons garlic powder

3 teaspoons dried, or 1 tablespoon chopped fresh, oregano

4 teaspoons kosher salt

2 teaspoons freshly ground black pepper

2/3 cup freshly grated Parmesan cheese

Soup

1   pound dried chickpeas

3   tablespoons olive oil

1   large Spanish onion, peeled and diced

2   carrots, peeled and sliced

3   ribs celery, diced

5   whole cloves garlic, peeled

3   quarts vegetable or chicken stock

Juice and zest of 2 lemons

1/4   cup tahini (sesame) paste

1   teaspoon dried mint leaves

1   teaspoon crushed red pepper flakes

1   teaspoon ground coriander

1   can (16 ounces) chickpeas, drained and rinsed

1   bunch scallions, minced

    Kosher salt and freshly ground black pepper, to taste

■ For the pita chips: Preheat the oven to 375 degrees. Using a sharp knife or carefully pulling with your hands, split each pita round in half horizontally, so you end up with two flat circles. Cut each circle into six triangles. Line two baking sheets with foil. Place the pita triangles on top, inside facing up. Using a pastry brush, brush the inside surface of each piece with olive oil. Sprinkle each with garlic powder, oregano, salt, pepper, and cheese. Bake for 8 to 10 minutes, or until lightly brown and crispy. Serve warm, or let cool and store in a resealable plastic bag. Makes 10 to 12 servings.

■ For the soup: Place the dried chickpeas in a deep bowl and add water to cover by 2

inches. Place in the refrigerator and soak overnight. Drain before using.

■ Heat a stockpot over medium-high heat. Add the olive oil, onion, carrots, celery, and garlic. Sauté for 10 minutes. Add the soaked chickpeas and stock. Bring to a boil. Reduce the heat to medium and simmer until the chickpeas are soft and tender, 1 to 1 1/4 hours. Add the lemon juice, lemon zest, tahini, mint, red pepper flakes, and coriander. Puree the soup in the pot using a hand blender or working in batches with a regular blender until smooth. Add the canned chickpeas, scallions, salt, and pepper. Stir to combine.

Makes 10 to 12 servings

Childhood Favorites

Aside from cough medicine, most children think everything tastes good on a spoon. This chapter celebrates some of the most soothing and nourishing nursery foods, including a tortellini variation on the classic chicken noodle soup. I also resurrected the alphabet soup and the vegetable soup that I adored when I was growing up. My daughter's favorite, sweet potato-barley, was a school cafeteria sensation that inspired a silly song. As a bonus, many of these soups turn vegetables into something more intriguing than the usual serving that gets pushed to the side of the plate.

As a child, I didn't spend a lot of time reading classics like *Johnny Tremain* and *The Lion, the Witch, and the Wardrobe.* It was cookbooks that held my interest, especially the ones with pictures. I would read the same ones, and I never grew tired of them. When my mom wasn't looking, I would pull her cookbooks from the kitchen shelf and spread them out on my pink and purple patchwork bedspread. One of my favorites was *A Treasury of Great Recipes* by Vincent and Mary Price. The authors visited all of the best and most famous restaurants in America, and printed the menus in the book. Vincent Price even wore the regional clothing from whatever country or state they were covering—and he certainly looked dashing.

I was especially infatuated with Betty Crocker's *Cooky Book* and *The Betty Crocker Boys and Girls Junior Cookbook.* As I looked at every picture over and over and over again, I imagined myself sitting with the children, drinking strawberry malts and eating sloppy Joes with a relish tray of carrots, olives, and celery on the side. Obviously, I did not quite fit in with the children around the neighborhood who did normal things like play kickball. It worried my mother. She would knock on my door and say, "Marj, how many times can you read those same cookbooks over and over again?" I replied by holding the books close to my chest, as if she were going to take them away.

As the years passed, I somehow lost track of my beloved *Cooky Book.* It was like losing touch with a great friend. My delight was incomparable when I recently found a copy while doing some holiday shopping. Though it was originally published in 1963, it had been such a popular book that it was reproduced with the exact same recipes and pictures. I was swooning. It was like reconnecting with a long-lost family member. I snapped up two copies just in case I lost a copy again.

Alphabet Soup

When my two sisters and I were growing up, we often asked our mom to make alphabet soup. We loved picking the letters from our spoons and spelling our names, or the names of the boys that we liked. Janie always wanted extra noodles in the batch, but Mom refused, telling us they would soak up all the broth. We didn't care, because the noodles were the best part. They were small, but still satisfyingly chewy. We also liked to crumble saltines into the soup for some crunch. I have added green beans, peas, and tomatoes to this recipe to painlessly sneak in a few healthy vegetables with the main attraction—the pasta.

8   cups chicken stock
5   carrots, peeled and sliced
2   ribs celery, sliced
2   potatoes, peeled and diced small
1   can (8 ounces) diced tomatoes, drained

1   cup green beans, trimmed and cut into 2-inch pieces
3/4 cup alphabet pasta
1/2 cup frozen peas
1   tablespoon minced fresh parsley
    Kosher salt, to taste

▪ In a stockpot add the stock and bring to a boil over high heat. Add the carrots, celery, potatoes, and tomatoes and return to a boil. Reduce the heat to medium and simmer for 20 minutes. Add the green beans and alphabet pasta, and continue cooking for 10 minutes.

▪ Add the frozen peas, parsley, and salt and cook until thoroughly heated.

Makes 8 to 10 servings

If your children are learning a foreign language, ask them to spell out basic words with the pasta letters. Not only does this give them a fun way to practice their new vocabulary, it also gives you a chance to learn, too. Just be prepared for them to laugh at your appalling mispronunciations.

Italian Vegetable Soup with Rice

I never seem to tire of this soup. Its richness comes from the different types of tomatoes in its base stock. The vegetables load it up with colorful flecks of orange, yellow, and green. It always reminds me of the Sunday afternoons when my mom cooked a large batch of vegetable soup for us to eat all day long. I enjoyed nothing more than sitting at our kitchen table eating bowl after bowl. I ate so much soup that when I stood up and walked, I could hear it swishing in my stomach.

3	tablespoons olive oil
1	large Spanish onion, peeled and diced
2	ribs celery, sliced
6	carrots, peeled and sliced
4	cloves garlic, minced
2	cans (16 ounces each) diced tomatoes
1	can (28 ounces) ground or crushed tomatoes
12	cups vegetable or chicken stock
4	cups tomato juice
1	can (16 ounces) chickpeas, drained and rinsed
1	can (16 ounces) kidney beans, drained and

	rinsed
2	bay leaves
2	medium zucchini, diced
2	medium summer squash, diced
1/3	cup uncooked white rice
1/2	cup frozen peas
1/2	bunch fresh basil leaves, torn into smaller pieces
2	teaspoons balsamic vinegar
	Kosher salt and freshly ground black pepper, to taste

■ Heat a stockpot over medium-high heat. Add the olive oil, onion, celery, carrots, and garlic. Sauté for 5 to 7 minutes, stirring frequently. Add the diced tomatoes, ground tomatoes, stock, tomato juice, chickpeas, kidney beans, and bay leaves. Bring to a boil. Reduce the heat to medium and simmer for 30 minutes.

■ Add the zucchini, summer squash, and rice. Return to a boil over medium-high heat. Reduce the heat to medium and simmer an additional 15 minutes. Add the peas, basil, balsamic vinegar, salt, and pepper and cook until thoroughly heated. Remove the bay leaves before serving.

Makes 10 to 12 servings

Sweet Potato, Chicken, and Barley Soup

photo on page 108

When my daughter, Emily, was a baby, she loved sweet potatoes so much that one day, when I went to lift her from her crib, her skin looked orange. I panicked, thinking she had hepatitis, but the doctor knew right away that I had just given her too many jars of sweet potatoes. She never lost her taste for this naturally sweet, creamy vegetable. When she got older, I made her this soup to take to school for lunch. When she opened her thermos, all her friends wanted to try this eye-catching, chunky array of chicken, vegetables, and barley pearls. They wrote a song about it called "Sweet Potato Chick Chick a Barley." Every time I start making this recipe, I can't shake that tune out of my head. Though Emily doesn't bring it for lunch everyday any more, it's still one of her favorites. At the shop, grown-ups like it, too.

3 tablespoons olive oil	2 bay leaves
3 cloves garlic, minced	4 large sweet potatoes, peeled and cut into chunks
1 Spanish onion, peeled and diced	
2 ribs celery, diced	3 cups chopped, cooked chicken
4 carrots, peeled and sliced	1/2 bunch fresh dill, chopped
3 parsnips, peeled and grated	1 tablespoon balsamic vinegar
1 1/4 cups pearl barley	Kosher salt and freshly ground black pepper, to taste
10 cups chicken stock	

■ Heat a stockpot over medium-high heat and add the olive oil. Add the garlic, onion, celery, and carrots. Sauté for 5 minutes, stirring occasionally. Add the parsnips, barley, stock, and bay leaves. Bring to a boil. Cover the pot and reduce the heat to medium. Simmer for 25 minutes.

■ Add the sweet potatoes and chicken and simmer for 20 minutes longer. Remove the bay leaves and discard. Remove from the heat and stir in the dill, vinegar, salt, and pepper.

Makes 12 servings

A child who is tired of the usual lunchbox fare of sandwiches and apples might appreciate varying the menu with soup. Start with a sturdy thermos. In the morning, when you are packing lunch, reheat the soup in the microwave and pour it into the thermos. Chilled soup can be poured right from the refrigerator into the Thermos. Make sure to include a spoon, a napkin, and fun garnishes to float in the soup, such as cheese cubes or goldfish-shaped crackers.

Chicken Tortellini Soup

Isn't it amazing how children will eat just about anything made with pasta? My daughter, Emily, would eat a bowlful of this soup every night if I let her. I have to admit that her preference comes in handy on those days when I am so tired that just the thought of cooking and grocery shopping makes me want to cry. This soup helps turn a meal of last resort into a real dinner.

12 cups water	1/2 bunch chopped fresh basil leaves
1 pound cheese tortellini	1/4 cup freshly grated Parmesan cheese, plus additional, for garnish
2 teaspoons olive oil	Pinch of crushed red pepper flakes
8 cups chicken stock or broth	Kosher salt and freshly ground black pepper, to taste
1 cup coarsely chopped cooked chicken	
2 cups baby spinach	

■ In an 8 to 10-quart stockpot bring the water to a boil over high heat. Add the tortellini and cook according to the package directions. Drain the pasta and rinse with cold water to stop the cooking. Place in a bowl, toss with the olive oil, and set aside.

■ In a stockpot bring the stock to a boil over high heat. Add the chicken and simmer for 3 minutes. Remove from the heat and add the cooked tortellini, baby spinach, basil, cheese, and red pepper flakes. Stir well and season with salt and pepper. Garnish with extra grated Parmesan cheese.

Makes 4 to 6 servings

Keep a package or two of tortellini tucked into your freezer so you can make this meal in a hurry. If you don't have fresh basil on hand, substitute parsley or cilantro.

Canadian Yellow Split Pea Soup with Smoked Shoulder of Pork

I had never tasted a smoked shoulder of pork until my mother-in-law, Rosemarie, served it to me. One bite made me realize that I had been missing out all of those years! I became hooked and had to try making it on my own. A shoulder of pork is also called a "picnic roast," and what a picnic it can make. I like to use the meat in sandwiches with black bread and mustard. Any kid who likes a hearty, old-fashioned bowl of pea soup is sure to appreciate this thick and hearty version.

1   cooked, smoked shoulder of pork, including the bone and 8 cups of stock (from Pasta Fagioli Soup on page 96)

6   tablespoons salted butter

2   cups diced Spanish onions

4   ribs celery, sliced

8   to 10 carrots, peeled and sliced

4   whole cloves garlic, peeled

1 1/2   pounds (24 ounces) dried yellow split peas

4   to 6 cups chicken stock

1   teaspoon ground bay leaves

2   cups cream sherry, divided

1   tablespoon balsamic vinegar

2   teaspoons Worcestershire sauce
    Kosher salt and freshly ground black pepper, to taste

■ Cut the smoked shoulder meat into bite-size pieces and set aside. In a stockpot melt the butter over medium-high heat. Add the onions, celery, carrots, and garlic. Sauté for 10 minutes. Add the pork bone, split peas, pork stock, chicken stock, bay leaves, and 1 cup of the sherry. Bring to a boil. Reduce the heat to medium. Cover the pot and simmer until the peas are tender and mushy. Remove the pork bone from the soup and discard.

Add the remaining cup of sherry, vinegar and Worcestershire sauce. Remove from the heat. Puree the soup in the pot using a hand blender or working in batches with a regular blender until smooth. Add salt and pepper. Stir in the reserved pork meat and return to the stove. Simmer over medium heat for an additional 5 to 7 minutes.

Makes 10 to 12 servings

Autumn Flavors

The first cool, crisp day of September feels like opening day at the New England Soup Factory. Autumn is our busiest season because people are finally ready for something heartier than the salads and iced tea that sustained them all summer. We anticipate with excitement the renewed rush of customers and the chance to prepare some of the soups that were rotated off the menu in order to make room for our chilled selections. In New England, the growing season is so short that there is always reason to celebrate the arrival of squash, tree-ripened pears and apples, mushrooms, freshly dug potatoes, and other treasures of the fall harvest. These soups take advantage of these seasonal ingredients. We especially like pumpkin because it's versatile enough to go with cranberries, yellow split peas, white beans—and our signature Thanksgiving soup: Pumpkin, Lobster, and Ginger. We also bring out spicy selections like our Tortilla and Butternut Squash Soup with Green Chilies, which tastes remarkably like a plate of nachos!

The year that Paul and I met while attending a culinary internship in Florida, he confided to me one day that he was sorry to be missing the autumn in New England. I thought he was nuts! Here we were wearing bathing suits and water skiing in October, and he wanted to go back to sweaters and fireplaces. Ignoring my reaction, Paul reminisced about the pleasures of the season's first apple cider and his mom's apple crisp pie. He missed picking out a pumpkin that would look just right on his front porch. More than anything, he was sorry that we were not going to be home for Thanksgiving. In fact, we had to work that day, as the resort was booked.

When we finally returned to Boston in December, I met his family for the first time. They invited me for Christmas dinner—another first for me, as I grew up celebrating Hanukkah. His mom went out of her way to make him an apple crisp pie because he had missed the season. She also made about eight other pies and cakes, plus dozens of cookies. No Pepperidge Farm in this house! As we were getting ready to leave that night, she handed me a big care package to take home to my parents and sisters. It was filled with homemade fudge with nuts, cookies, slices of cakes and pies, peanut brittle, and her famous Sicilian-style priolata sausage bread. I was astounded by how much food she made for Christmas, and how she remembered that Paul hadn't tasted an apple pie all autumn long. At last, I understood why he was sad to miss an autumn back home. Now his mom is part of my family, too, and I still appreciate her spirit of celebration, and how she savors each season's bounty.

Apple, Onion, and Cheddar Soup

This soup is perfect for a Sunday open-house party during the cool fall months. It incorporates apples and cheese, which are also an old-fashioned combination for a pie in New England. The soup builds contrasting layers of sweetness, starting with the apple cider in the stock. Into that go the onions, sautéed slowly until they are perfectly browned and sweet. Green apples add tartness. For a memorable menu, serve Black Forest Ham Sandwiches (see page 204) along with the soup.

3 tablespoons butter

2 cloves garlic, minced

5 large Spanish onions, peeled and thinly sliced

4 Granny Smith apples, peeled and sliced

6 cups chicken stock

2 cups apple cider

2 teaspoons caraway seeds

1/2 teaspoon dried thyme leaves

1 cup heavy cream

2 cups grated sharp cheddar cheese

1/4 cup freshly grated Parmesan cheese

2 tablespoons Calvados (apple brandy)

   Kosher salt and freshly ground black pepper, to taste

■ In a stockpot melt the butter over medium heat. Add the garlic and onions. Sauté for 25 minutes, or until the onions are soft and golden. Add the sliced apples and sauté an additional 5 minutes. Add the chicken stock, apple cider, caraway seeds, and thyme. Bring to a boil over medium-high heat. Reduce the heat to medium, cover the pot, and simmer for 35 to 40 minutes.

■ Remove the pot from the stove. Add the cream, cheddar cheese, and Parmesan cheese. Stir until the cheeses melt completely. Add the Calvados and season with salt and pepper. Return to the stove and simmer an additional 3 minutes.

Makes 12 servings

⊙ Farmers' Root Vegetable Soup

As much as I love the deep, rich flavor of chicken, sometimes I want just chunks of vegetables without the meat. Root vegetables have a strong, unmistakably earthy identity. They cost relatively little, but their rich, concentrated flavor makes them seem expensive. Carrots and the garnet yams (an orange-red variety) give this soup a royal glow. If you can't find garnet yams, substitute regular yams or sweet potatoes. This is one of the easiest recipes I make—once you cut the vegetables, the soup just simmers until it's done. When you sit down to eat, you feel like you're digging into a big bowl of edible jewels.

1 large Spanish onion, peeled and diced	3 cups turnips, peeled and diced into chunks
2 ribs celery, diced	1 bulb celeriac (celery root), peeled and cut into chunks
1 bulb fennel, diced	
6 carrots, peeled and diced	14 cups chicken or vegetable stock
3 large garnet yams, peeled and diced into chunks	1 bunch fresh dill, chopped
3 parsnips, peeled and sliced	Kosher salt and freshly ground black pepper, to taste

■ Place the onion, celery, fennel, carrots, yams, parsnips, turnips, and celeriac in a large stockpot. Add the stock. Bring to a boil over high heat. Reduce the heat to medium and simmer for 45 to 50 minutes. Remove from the heat. Add the dill, salt, and pepper.

Makes 10 to 12 servings

Garnet yams are an orange-red variety also sometimes called red yams. I am partial to their bright color in this soup. The yam and the sweet potato are often confused with one another, but they come from entirely different plants. What they do have in common is their sweet and starchy properties, which makes them fairly interchangeable in recipes. In this soup, you could substitute any type of yam or sweet potato if you can't find the garnets.

Potato, Bacon, and Chive Soup with Horseradish

In this recipe, I tried to sneak all of my favorite potato toppings into a soup. Horseradish proved irresistible, as it is so delicious with whipped potatoes. I also used the crumbled bacon and chives that I would normally sprinkle on top of baked potatoes. Naturally, I had to throw in some sour cream, too. Somehow, everything ended up tasting fantastic together. Roast Beef Sandwiches (see page 202) make a good accompaniment.

3   tablespoons butter

4   whole cloves garlic, peeled

1   large Spanish onion, peeled and diced

2   ribs celery, sliced

8   Yukon Gold potatoes, peeled and cut into chunks

6   cups chicken stock

2   teaspoons onion powder

2   teaspoons garlic powder

1   cup sour cream

2   cups light cream

4   tablespoons bottled minced white horseradish

4   dashes Worcestershire sauce

4   dashes Tabasco sauce

1   cup crumbled cooked bacon (reserve some, for garnish)

1   bunch fresh chives, sliced small (reserve some, for garnish)

    Kosher salt and freshly ground black pepper, to taste

■ In a stockpot melt the butter over medium-high heat. Add the garlic, onion, and celery. Sauté for 7 minutes. Add the potatoes and stir to coat with the butter and vegetables. Add the chicken stock, onion powder, and garlic powder. Bring to a boil. Reduce the heat to medium and simmer until the potatoes are soft and tender, 30 to 35 minutes. Remove from the stove. Puree the soup in the pot using a hand blender or working in batches with a regular blender until smooth and creamy. Add the sour cream, light cream, horseradish, Worcestershire sauce, and Tabasco sauce. Puree once again until everything is incorporated. Return the pot to the stove. Add the bacon, chives, salt, and pepper. Simmer an additional 5 minutes. Garnish each serving with crumbled bacon and chives.

Makes 10 to 12 servings

Creamy Wild Mushroom Bisque

Mushrooms play a starring role in our kitchen during the autumn months. We look for specialty varieties, such as floppy-brimmed shiitakes, trumpet-shaped chanterelles, and feathery-looking hen of the woods. I like to use a combination of wild mushrooms in this bisque. It makes an appealing first course for an elegant Thanksgiving or Christmas meal.

1   tablespoon salted butter

3   whole cloves garlic

1   large Spanish onion, peeled and diced

1   cup diced celery

1   pound shiitake mushrooms

2   large portobello mushrooms

1/4 pound chanterelle mushrooms

2   to 3 large Yukon Gold potatoes, peeled and quartered

6   cups homemade chicken stock

2   teaspoons fresh thyme leaves

1   cup light cream

    Kosher salt and freshly ground black pepper, to taste

2   tablespoons dry sherry

2   teaspoons Worcestershire sauce

1   tablespoon olive oil

■ Melt the butter in a stockpot over medium-high heat. Add the garlic, onion, and celery. Sauté for 8 minutes. Slice the shiitake, portobello, and chanterelle mushrooms, setting aside a total of 1/2 cup of mixed mushrooms for the garnish. Add the remaining mushrooms and the potatoes to the stockpot. Sauté for 5 minutes. Add the stock and bring to a boil. Lower the heat to medium and simmer until the potatoes are tender, 30 to 35 minutes. Remove from the heat. Add the thyme and puree in the pot using a hand blender or working in batches in a regular blender until smooth. Add the cream, salt and pepper, sherry, and Worcestershire sauce. Stir well.

■ Heat the olive oil in a small sauté pan over medium-high heat. Add the reserved 1/2 cup mushrooms and sauté until soft, about 10 minutes. Season with salt and pepper. Add the mushrooms into the soup and stir to incorporate.

Makes 8 to 10 servings

Black Bean and Sausage Soup

This soup's deep black color makes it ideal for Halloween. I make a big pot to serve after dark, when everyone in our house is exhausted after a long night of trick or treating.

1 pound dried black beans	16 cups chicken or beef stock
1 pound sweet Italian sausage	1 can (6 ounces) tomato paste
1 pound hot Italian sausage	2 teaspoons fennel seeds
3 tablespoons olive oil	1 cup sherry
4 cloves garlic, minced	6 dashes Worcestershire sauce
1 large Spanish onion, peeled and diced	1/4 teaspoon crushed red pepper flakes
6 carrots, peeled and sliced	1 tablespoon balsamic vinegar
3 ribs celery, sliced	Kosher salt and freshly ground black pepper, to taste

■ Place the beans in a large, deep bowl. Add enough water to cover by 2 inches. Place in the refrigerator and soak overnight. Drain before using.

■ Preheat the oven to 350 degrees. Line a baking sheet or a roasting pan with parchment paper or foil. Place the sausages on the pan and bake for 25 minutes. Let cool on a plate lined with paper towels. Cut into 1/4 to 1/2-inch slices and set aside.

■ Heat a stockpot over medium-high heat. Add the olive oil, garlic, onion, carrots, and celery. Sauté for 10 minutes. Add the black beans and sauté an additional 5 minutes. Add the stock, tomato paste, and fennel seeds and bring to a boil. Reduce the heat to medium and simmer for 11/4 hours, or until the beans are very tender. Remove from the heat. Puree the soup in the pot using a hand blender or working in batches with a regular blender until very smooth. Return the pot to the stove. Add the sherry, sausage slices, Worcestershire sauce, red pepper flakes, vinegar, salt, and pepper. Simmer an additional 10 minutes.

Makes 10 to 12 servings

This soup goes well with grilled muenster cheese sandwiches topped with a few slices of jalapeño peppers for added spark.

Spicy Chickpea and Butternut Squash Soup

This has always been our most popular vegetarian soup. Made with coconut milk, lime juice, tomatoes, and ginger, it's hot, sweet, sour, and luscious all in the same bite. Our shops in Boston are near some of the best colleges and universities around. Many of the students who come in are vegetarians with diverse and eclectic tastes, and this seems to satisfy them.

3 tablespoons olive oil	1/2 cup soy sauce
1 large Spanish onion, peeled and diced	1/4 cup freshly squeezed lime juice
4 carrots, peeled and sliced	1 tablespoon ground ginger
1/2 cup diced celery	1 tablespoon ground coriander
4 cloves garlic, minced	1 cup flaked coconut
1 pound butternut squash, peeled and diced into chunks	1/2 cup packed brown sugar
2 cups (16 ounces) canned diced tomatoes	1 can (14 ounces) coconut milk
2 cups (16 ounces) canned chickpeas, rinsed and drained	1 teaspoon minced Scotch bonnet chile pepper (see note)
12 cups vegetable stock	1/2 bunch fresh cilantro leaves, chopped
2 cups tomato juice	Kosher salt and freshly ground black pepper, to taste

■ Heat a stockpot over medium-high heat. Add the olive oil, onion, carrots, celery, and garlic. Sauté for 10 minutes. Add the butternut squash and sauté an additional 5 minutes. Add the tomatoes, chickpeas, stock, tomato juice, soy sauce, lime juice, ginger, coriander, coconut, and brown sugar. Bring to a boil.

Reduce the heat to medium and simmer until the squash is tender, 35 to 40 minutes.

■ Remove from the heat and add the coconut milk, chile pepper, cilantro, salt, and pepper.

Makes 12 servings

Scotch bonnet chile peppers are loaded with heat and an exotic flavor and aroma. A close cousin is the habanero pepper. You may substitute bottled habanero hot sauce (available at supermarkets and Caribbean specialty shops) if you cannot find fresh Scotch bonnet peppers.

Pumpkin and Cranberry Soup

Each year we wait to make this soup until the air is crisp and everyone is reinvigorated by the bustle of the new school year. The first batch feels like Opening Day for the fall. The flaming orange color and creamy, dense texture make it a luscious treat. For a finishing flourish, we toss in dried cranberries that have been soaked in sherry. Each spoonful looks like it's studded with polka dots.

1 cup dried cranberries	1 can (16 ounces) pumpkin puree
1/2 cup cream sherry	8 cups chicken stock
3 tablespoons butter	3 tablespoons dark brown sugar
1 large Spanish onion, peeled and diced	1/2 cup pure maple syrup (do not use imitation)
2 ribs celery, diced	1/4 teaspoon ground nutmeg
5 carrots, peeled and sliced	1 cup heavy cream
2 pounds fresh pumpkin or butternut squash, peeled and cut into chunks	Kosher salt and freshly ground black pepper, to taste

■ Place the cranberries in a glass or ceramic bowl and add the sherry. Cover the bowl and let the cranberries soak for at least 2 hours or overnight.

■ In a stockpot melt the butter over medium-high heat. Add the onion, celery, and carrots. Sauté for 5 minutes. Add the fresh pumpkin and sauté for 5 minutes longer. Add the pumpkin puree, stock, brown sugar, maple syrup, and nutmeg. Bring to a boil. Reduce the heat to medium and simmer for 35 to 40 minutes, or until the pumpkin is soft and tender. Remove from the heat and puree with a blender or hand blender until the soup is smooth and creamy. Add the cream and the cranberries with their soaking liquid. Season with salt and pepper and stir well.

Makes 12 servings

Tortilla and Butternut Squash Soup

photo on
page 118

I came up with the idea for this recipe while vacationing in Aruba. When I tasted a soup similar to this one, I begged the waiter to tell me a few of the ingredients because it seemed like the type of thing I just had to add to my menu. He told me that squash was the base and that the chefs pureed tortilla chips into the broth. That was all I needed to hear. My version tastes like a big plate of nachos.

3 tablespoons salted butter	8 ounces salted tortilla chips
3 cloves garlic, minced	1/2 cup fresh cilantro leaves
2 cups diced onions	2 cups shredded Monterey Jack cheese
3 carrots, sliced	1 can (4 ounces) diced green chilies
3 ribs celery, sliced	1 bunch scallions, sliced
1 pound butternut squash, peeled and diced	2 tablespoons freshly squeezed lime juice
12 cups chicken stock	8 dashes green Tabasco sauce
1 cup sherry	Freshly ground black pepper, to taste

■ In a large stockpot melt the butter over medium-high heat. Add the garlic, onions, carrots, celery, and butternut squash. Sauté for 10 minutes, stirring frequently. Add the stock and sherry. Bring to a boil. Reduce the heat to medium and simmer until the squash is soft and tender, 35 to 40 minutes. Remove from the heat and stir in the tortilla chips until wilted. Add the cilantro and cheese and let the cheese melt into the soup. Puree the soup in the pot using a hand blender or working in batches with a regular blender until completely smooth. Add the chilies and scallions. Stir to combine. Season with lime juice, Tabasco sauce, and black pepper. Return to the stove and simmer an additional 5 minutes.

Makes 12 to 14 servings

For a festive presentation, serve this soup in deep, wide, colorful bowls. Sprinkle with blue corn tortilla chips, chunks of avocado, sliced scallions, and a sprinkle of Monterey Jack cheese. Serve a wedge of lime on the side of the bowl.

Ⓥ Yellow Split Pea Soup with Pumpkin

This soup, retired for the summer, goes right back onto our menu as soon as the fall harvest hits the markets. The comforting flavor of thick pea soup is enhanced with the natural sweetness of the fresh pumpkin. If you stock your pantry with the basic ingredients, you can make this the day you drive past a farm stand and spontaneously decide it's time to stop for a pumpkin.

3	tablespoons butter	1	pound dried yellow split peas
1	large Spanish onion, peeled and diced	16	cups chicken or vegetable stock
6	carrots, peeled and sliced	2	teaspoons Worcestershire sauce
3	ribs celery, sliced	5	dashes Tabasco sauce
4	whole cloves garlic, peeled	1/2	bunch fresh dill sprigs
1 1/2	pounds pumpkin or squash, peeled and cut into chunks		Kosher salt and freshly ground black pepper, to taste

■ In a stockpot melt the butter over medium-high heat. Add the onion, carrots, celery, garlic, and pumpkin. Sauté for 10 minutes. Add the split peas and cook an additional 5 minutes. Pour in the stock and bring to a boil. Reduce the heat to medium, cover the pot, and simmer for 1 hour, or until the split peas are tender. Remove from the heat and add the Worcestershire sauce, Tabasco sauce, dill, salt, and pepper. Puree in the pot using a hand blender or working in batches with a regular blender until smooth.

Makes 8 to 10 servings

Because the texture of this soup is smooth and creamy, I like to serve roasted pumpkin seeds on top of the soup for crunch. You can often find the greenish, Mexican-style seeds, called pepitas, at a Latin American market or natural foods store. It's also easy to roast your own seeds if you are scooping out a pumpkin. Reserve the seeds, then wash and spread them out to dry on paper towels. Preheat the oven to 375 degrees and line a baking sheet with foil or parchment paper. Spread the seeds in a single layer on a baking sheet, drizzle with 2 tablespoons of olive oil, plus Kosher salt, and garlic powder to taste. Bake for 7 to 10 minutes until lightly brown. Let cool before adding to the soup.

Pumpkin and White Bean Soup

This is my favorite pumpkin soup recipe. I created it after I had eaten a magnificent butternut squash ravioli with brown butter and sage at Olives restaurant near Boston, chef-owner Todd English's home base. I had to see if I could make a soup that could remind me of its perfectly balanced flavors. I played with the spices and ingredients, and found that white beans gave me better results than pasta. Whenever I taste this soup, it reminds me of that meal at Olives. I am thankful to Chef Todd for inspiring me to create bold and spirited dishes.

2 1/2 pounds pumpkin, peeled and cut into 3/4-inch cubes, divided

1 1/2 tablespoons olive oil

Kosher salt and freshly ground black pepper, to taste

4 tablespoons butter

4 whole cloves garlic, peeled

1 large Spanish onion, peeled and chopped

2 ribs celery, diced

5 carrots, peeled and sliced

10 cups chicken stock

1/2 teaspoon rubbed sage

1/2 teaspoon ground nutmeg

1/2 cup packed brown sugar

1/2 cup freshly grated Parmesan cheese, plus additional, for garnish

1/2 cup cream sherry

Kosher salt and freshly ground black pepper, to taste

2 cups cooked cannellini beans

1/4 cup torn fresh basil leaves, for garnish

■ Preheat the oven to 425 degrees. Place 3 cups of the pumpkin in a roasting pan. Drizzle with the olive oil and season with salt and pepper. Bake for 25 to 30 minutes, or until soft and brown on the outer edges. Set aside.

■ Melt the butter in a stockpot over medium-high heat. Add the garlic, onion, celery, and carrots. Sauté for 5 minutes. Add the remaining pumpkin and sauté for an additional 5 minutes. Add the stock, sage, and nutmeg. Bring to a boil. Reduce the heat to medium, cover the pot, and simmer for 30 to 35 minutes, or until the vegetables are soft and tender. Remove from the heat and add the brown sugar, cheese, and sherry. Puree the soup in the pot using a hand blender or working in batches with a regular blender until smooth. Season with salt and pepper. Add the cannellini beans and the reserved roasted pumpkin chunks. Stir well. Serve in big, deep bowls with the basil leaves and freshly shaved Parmesan cheese.

Makes 12 to 14 servings

Pumpkin, Lobster, and Ginger Soup

This soup really captures the essence of autumn in New England. It has become a signature on our Thanksgiving menu because it makes such a distinctive first course. Sweet and creamy pumpkin simmered in lobster stock gives the soup its strength and body. Fresh ginger and crème fraîche spark it up. Sweet nuggets of fresh lobster—a treat in any season—are dispersed throughout. I first served this soup at a luncheon for 300 at a national Women Chefs and Restaurateurs conference held in Boston. We garnished each little bowl with toasted pumpkin seeds, fresh chives, and a drizzle of crème fraîche and received rave reviews from a highly critical audience!

3	tablespoons salted butter	1	cup white wine
2	whole cloves garlic, peeled	1	tablespoon Worcestershire sauce
1	Spanish onion, peeled and diced	3	tablespoons brown sugar
2	carrots, peeled and sliced	2	cups heavy cream
2	ribs celery, sliced	1	cup crème fraîche
2	tablespoons grated fresh ginger	3/4	cup cream sherry
2	pounds fresh pumpkin, peeled and cut into chunks	2	cups coarsely chopped cooked lobster meat
2	quarts lobster stock		Kosher salt and freshly ground black pepper, to taste
1	can (16 ounces) pumpkin puree	1/3	cup toasted pumpkin seeds, for garnish

■ In a stockpot melt the butter over medium-high heat. Add the garlic, onion, carrots, celery, ginger, and fresh pumpkin. Sauté for 15 minutes. Add the stock, pumpkin puree, and wine. Bring to a boil. Reduce the heat to medium and simmer until the pumpkin is tender and soft, 25 to 30 minutes.

■ Add the Worcestershire sauce, brown sugar, cream, crème fraîche, and sherry. Puree the soup in the pot using a hand blender or working in batches with a regular blender until smooth. Stir in the lobster meat and season with salt and pepper. Garnish each serving with toasted pumpkin seeds.

Makes 8 to 10 servings

Winter's Brew

These soups and stews warm your kitchen when icicles hang from your eaves and the lawn has disappeared under snowdrifts. This is the time for hearty flavors and starchy root vegetables. In this chapter, you can find classic beef stew for a Sunday supper and chili for a Super Bowl party. Even the harsh-tasting turnip and the gnarly celeriac root can be transformed into a smooth, creamy puree that gives you a boost on an icy day. Some of these recipes need to simmer for a long time, but do you really want to bundle up and venture outside anyway?

When I was a child, my mother always made enough beef stew in her orange Le Creuset Dutch oven to last for what seemed like the entire winter. I got so I dreaded seeing that pot come out of the oven because it meant leftovers. Mom and Dad didn't care how many times we ate it because they liked it better each time.

By the time I went off to culinary school, I never wanted to see beef stew again, and I always avoided it. Then I found myself married and living in a rented, two-family house with a new baby. It snowed all winter long, Paul had to keep going out to shovel. I wanted to make something that would cheer him up when he came back in with red cheeks and snow trailing from his boots. Reaching back into my repertoire, I realized that my mother's old standby, beef stew, would do the trick. Paul relished every bite—and, though I had once vowed never to keep recycling leftovers, we ended up eating it for days. I realized that my parents had been right all along. It did taste better every time we warmed it up.

Mushroom Lentil Soup

This soup is a hearty blend of brown lentils, vegetables, and a variety of mushrooms. I love the texture because each bite is wonderfully chewy. The scallions, parsley, and thyme finish it with a burst of green crunchiness. This is my dad's favorite soup. I always drop off a quart for him the day I make it. I usually check later to see how he and my mom liked it, but then I learn that my mom never even got one bite of it!

3   tablespoons olive oil
3   cloves garlic, minced
1   Spanish onion, peeled and diced
2   ribs celery, diced
6   carrots, peeled and diced or sliced
2   portobello mushroom caps, diced
1/4 pound shiitake mushrooms, sliced
1/4 pound oyster mushrooms, sliced
1/2 pound dried lentils

1   cup dry sherry
8   cups beef stock
2   bay leaves
1   tablespoon chopped fresh thyme
1/4 cup chopped fresh parsley
1   bunch scallions, sliced
1   tablespoon sherry vinegar
    Kosher salt and freshly ground black pepper, to taste

■ Heat a stockpot over medium-high heat. Add the olive oil, garlic, onion, celery, and carrots. Sauté for 7 minutes. Add the portobello, shiitake, and oyster mushrooms. Sauté an additional 3 minutes. Add the lentils, sherry, stock, and bay leaves. Bring to a boil. Reduce the heat to medium and simmer for 1 1/4 hours.

■ Remove from the heat and discard the bay leaves. Add the thyme, parsley, scallions, vinegar, salt, and pepper. Stir well.

Makes 8 servings

Puree of Root Vegetable Soup

This has become one of our classic cold-weather soups. I usually make the first batch of the season in October, but I start getting phone calls for it in late September, followed by e-mails to our website asking when we will have it. It's a sweet, rich soup that tastes best after the first frost. In terms of comfort food, this soup is right up there with mashed potatoes. It includes wonderful, old-fashioned ingredients like turnips and celeriac. People who think that they do not like these vegetables are surprised to fall in love with them when they taste this soup. It must be the smooth, creamy texture of all the ingredients blended together.

3   tablespoons butter

3   whole cloves garlic, peeled

1   large Spanish onion, peeled and diced

2   ribs celery, diced

4   carrots, peeled and sliced

4   parsnips, peeled and sliced

1   large turnip or rutabaga, peeled and cut into chunks

2   sweet potatoes, peeled and cut into chunks

1   bulb celeriac, peeled and cut into chunks

12 cups chicken or vegetable stock

1/2 teaspoon ground nutmeg

2   cups light cream

    Kosher salt and freshly ground black pepper, to taste

■ In a stockpot melt the butter over medium-high heat. Add the garlic, onion, celery, carrots, and parsnips. Sauté for 5 to 8 minutes, stirring frequently. Add the turnip, sweet potatoes, celeriac, and stock. Bring to a boil. Reduce the heat to medium and simmer until the vegetables are soft and tender, about 40 minutes.

■ Remove from heat and add the nutmeg. Puree the soup in the pot with a hand blender or working in batches in a regular blender until smooth. Add the cream. Season with salt and pepper. Stir to combine. If the soup seems too thick, adjust the texture with additional stock or water.

Makes 8 to 10 servings

Turnips and rutabagas are close root vegetable cousins and can be used interchangeably in this recipe. At one time, turnips were disdained as food for the poor because they were also commonly used as cattle fodder. Now, their firm texture and slightly sharp flavor (they are part of the mustard family) make a great addition to a soup. Look for peeled turnips or rutabagas at the supermarket to shorten prep time.

Country Split Pea Soup with Bacon and Potatoes

I like my pea soups thick and hearty, and this peasant-style recipe certainly fills the bill. It's inexpensive to make, and I usually have all the ingredients on hand in my pantry at home. Make it a day ahead so the bacon has time to flavor the soup. To dress it up a little, serve it with a basket of freshly baked crostini.

3 tablespoons butter	2 tablespoons dry sherry
1 large Spanish onion, peeled and diced	5 dashes Tabasco sauce
2 ribs celery, sliced	2 cooked Yukon Gold potatoes, peeled and diced
8 large carrots, peeled and sliced	
3 whole cloves garlic, peeled	12 slices bacon, cooked until crisp (reserve some for garnish)
1 pound dried green split peas	
10 cups chicken stock	Kosher salt and freshly ground black pepper, to taste

■ Melt the butter in a 6 to 8-quart pot over medium-high heat. Add the onion, celery, carrots, and garlic. Sauté for 7 to 10 minutes, stirring frequently. Add the split peas and chicken stock. Bring to a boil. Reduce the heat to medium. Simmer for 1 hour, or until the split peas are soft and tender.

■ Remove from the stove. Add the sherry and Tabasco sauce. Puree the soup in the pot using a hand blender or working in batches with a regular blender until smooth. Add the cooked potatoes and bacon. Stir to combine thoroughly. Garnish each bowl with crumbled bacon.

Makes 8 to 10 servings

Sausage Minestrone Soup with Orzo

Everyone seems to love minestrone soup, maybe because it's such a celebration of vegetables in one bowl. In this recipe, the meaty flavor from the sausages really enhances the tomato-flavored stock. To keep the flavors balanced, I always use a combination of hot and sweet Italian sausages. If you have access to a butcher who makes the sausages in-house, your soup will taste even better. The addition of the orzo pasta near the end of the cooking time keeps it from swelling too much in the soup.

1	pound sweet Italian sausage
1	pound hot Italian sausage
3	tablespoons olive oil
1	large Spanish onion, peeled and diced
3	cloves garlic, minced
2	ribs celery, sliced
5	carrots, peeled and sliced
1	can (28 ounces) whole tomatoes, cut into pieces
12	cups chicken stock, plus additional as needed
4	cups tomato juice
2	bay leaves
1	can (16 ounces) chickpeas, drained and rinsed
1	can (16 ounces) dark red kidney beans, drained and rinsed
1	can (16 ounces) cannellini beans, drained and rinsed
1	large zucchini, diced
1	large summer squash, diced
1/2	cup dried orzo
3	tablespoons chopped fresh basil
	Kosher salt and freshly ground black pepper, to taste

■ Preheat the oven to 350 degrees. Line a baking sheet or a roasting pan with parchment paper or foil. Place the sausages on the pan and bake for 25 minutes. Let cool on a plate lined with paper towels. Cut into 1/4 to 1/2-inch slices.

■ Heat a stockpot over medium-high heat. Add the olive oil, onion, garlic, celery, and carrots. Sauté for 8 minutes. Add the tomatoes, stock, tomato juice, bay leaves, chickpeas, kidney beans, cannellini beans, and cooked sausage slices. Bring to a boil. Reduce the heat to medium, cover the pot, and simmer for 40 minutes, adding more stock or water if too much liquid evaporates. Remove and discard the bay leaves. Add the zucchini, summer squash, and orzo. Cook for an additional 10 minutes. Stir in the basil, salt, and pepper.

Makes 10 to 12 servings

It's important to cook the sausage separately so that you can drain a lot of its excess fat before you mix it into the soup.

Beef and Barley Soup

One of the most requested flavors of soup has to be beef and barley. It seems to be the ultimate in comfort food for toddlers, grandparents, and all ages in between. Make a batch in the middle of February when your bones feel cold and worn. In this recipe, you need to cook the meat separately to tenderize it and bring out the best in its flavor. (For a mushroom variation see page 151). A nice, crusty rye bread makes a great accompaniment.

Beef

- 3 pounds stew beef, cut into bite-size pieces
- 1/2 cup red wine vinegar
- 12 cups water
- 2 teaspoons kosher salt

Soup

- 3 tablespoons olive oil
- 3 cloves garlic, minced
- 1 large Spanish onion, peeled and diced
- 2 ribs celery, diced
- 6 carrots, peeled and sliced or diced
- Cooked stew beef (from recipe)
- 1/2 pound pearl barley
- 1 cup Burgundy wine
- 1 can (8 ounces) tomato paste
- 8 cups beef stock or broth
- 2 bay leaves
- 5 dashes Worcestershire sauce
- 1/4 cup chopped fresh parsley
- Kosher salt and freshly ground black pepper, to taste

■ For the beef: Place the beef, vinegar, water, and salt in an 8 to 10-quart stockpot. Bring to a boil over medium-high heat. Reduce the heat to medium and simmer for 1 1/2 hours. Drain and reserve.

■ For the soup: Heat a stockpot over medium-high heat. Add the olive oil, garlic, onion, celery, and carrots. Sauté for 7 minutes, stirring frequently. Add the cooked beef, barley, wine, tomato paste, stock, and bay leaves. Bring to a boil. Reduce the heat to medium and simmer, stirring every 15 minutes, for 1 1/4 hours. Remove from heat and add the Worcestershire sauce, parsley, salt, and pepper. Remove and discard the bay leaves before serving.

Makes 8 to 10 servings

Wild Mushroom and Barley Soup

This hearty soup updates the recipe that many of us remember, unhappily, as a bowl of brown mush. Instead of those blah button mushrooms, I decided to use portobellos, shiitakes, chanterelles, and enokis. Each type contributes a different texture. I also enriched the basic stock with tomato paste and red wine. Best of all, I cook the barley for no more than an hour, which leaves it with some spring in its bite.

2	tablespoons olive oil
2	cloves garlic, minced
1 1/2	cups diced onions
1 1/2	cups sliced or diced carrots
1/2	cup diced celery
3	large portobello mushrooms, diced
1	cup sliced shiitake mushrooms
1	cup sliced chanterelle mushrooms
1 1/2	cups pearl barley

2 1/2	quarts chicken or beef stock
2	cups Burgundy wine
1	teaspoon dried oregano
1	teaspoon dried basil
3	tablespoons tomato paste
1	cup enoki mushrooms
2	teaspoons balsamic vinegar
	Kosher salt and freshly ground black pepper, to taste

■ Heat a stockpot over medium-high heat. Add the olive oil and garlic. Stir quickly, then add the onions, carrots, and celery. Sauté for 5 minutes. Add the portabellas, shiitakes, and chanterelles. Sauté for 5 minutes more. Add the barley, stock, Burgundy, oregano, basil, and tomato paste. Stir well to combine. Bring to a boil. Reduce the heat to medium and simmer 45 minutes to 1 hour.

■ Remove from the heat. Stir in the enoki mushrooms and season with vinegar, salt, and pepper.

Makes 10 to 12 servings

Hearty and Rich Beef Stew

This recipe is a fixture on the New England Soup Factory from Columbus Day through Memorial Day. At home, beef stew makes a perfect Sunday meal. Start your preparations early, put it in the oven, and let it cook slowly until the flavor deepens and the meat is tender enough to fall apart. It's even better served over a bed of buttered wide noodles or pappardelle pasta tossed in a bit of fresh parsley.

2 1/2 pounds stew beef, cut into bite-sized pieces

3 cups flour seasoned with salt and pepper, to taste

4 tablespoons olive oil

3 cloves garlic, minced

1 pound fresh baby carrots

1 pound fresh pearl onions, peeled or 1 pound frozen pearl onions

10 small red bliss potatoes, cut into quarters

3 cups beef stock or broth

2 cups (16 ounces) canned ground or crushed tomatoes

1 bottle (750 milliliters) Burgundy or another fruity red wine, divided

2 bay leaves

1 teaspoon dried basil

1 cup frozen peas

Kosher salt and freshly ground black pepper, to taste

■ Preheat the oven to 325 degrees. Coat the stew beef with the seasoned flour. Heat the olive oil in a Dutch oven or braising pan over high heat. Add the meat, a few pieces at a time. Cook, turning several times with tongs, until the meat is crispy and brown on all sides. Repeat until all the meat is cooked. Set aside.

■ In the same pan, add the garlic, carrots, fresh onions if using, and potatoes. Sauté over medium-high heat for 5 minutes. Add the browned meat, stock, tomatoes, 2 cups of the red wine, bay leaves, and basil. Cover the pot, place in the oven, and bake for 1 hour. Remove from oven and add the remaining red wine. Bake, covered, for 3 hours more, or until the stew is fork tender. Remove from the oven. Remove and discard the bay leaves. Add the frozen peas and frozen onions, if using, and season with salt and pepper. Stir gently to combine.

Makes 8 servings

Chili Con Carne

photo on
page 138

I like my chili full-flavored and zesty, but you can control the heat by adding as much or as little chili powder and Tabasco sauce as you want. This chili is incredibly popular, especially during football season. People come and buy gallons at a time for their playoff and Super Bowl parties.

3   tablespoons olive oil

4   cloves garlic, minced

2   Spanish onions, peeled and diced

1   red bell pepper, seeded and diced into 3/4-inch pieces

1   yellow bell pepper, seeded and diced into 3/4-inch pieces

2   pounds ground beef chuck

2   cans (16 ounces each) dark red kidney beans, drained and rinsed

4   cups (32 ounces) canned ground or crushed tomatoes

2   cups tomato juice

2   cups beef or chicken stock or broth

1   tablespoon chili powder

1   tablespoon ground cumin

2   teaspoons dried oregano

2   teaspoons dried basil

1   tablespoon balsamic vinegar

6   to 8 dashes Tabasco sauce

Kosher salt and freshly ground black pepper, to taste

■ Heat a stockpot over medium-high heat. Add the olive oil, garlic, onions, and bell peppers. Sauté for 7 minutes. Add the ground beef and cook, stirring frequently, until the meat is browned, about 10 minutes. Add the kidney beans, tomatoes, tomato juice, stock, chili powder, cumin, oregano, and basil. Bring to a boil. Reduce the heat to medium and simmer for 1 1/2 hours. Season with vinegar, Tabasco sauce, salt, and pepper.

Makes 6 to 8 servings

Nothing beats a bowl of chili topped with shredded cheddar cheese and sour cream, but you can also use chili to enhance other dishes. We serve it in nacho salads. During baseball season, we also use it as a topping for foot-long long hot dogs—a messy but fun treat.

ⓥ Vegetarian White Bean Chili

This thick, zesty chili is loaded with white beans and a colorful confetti of vegetables. As the tomato and stock-based liquid simmers, the beans and chunks of carrots and bell peppers absorb the fragrant mix of spices. You might think that this recipe would appeal only to vegetarians, but we sell plenty of it to meat eaters as well. It's like a big bowl of spicy beans. Who wouldn't love that? For an entrée, spoon each serving over freshly steamed white or brown rice.

1   pound dried great northern beans

1/2 pound dried chickpeas

4   tablespoons olive oil

5   cloves garlic, minced

1   large Spanish onion, peeled and diced

4   carrots, peeled and diced into 3/4-inch pieces

1   yellow bell pepper, seeded and diced into 3/4-inch pieces

1   orange or red bell pepper, seeded and diced into 3/4-inch pieces

3   cups (24 ounces) canned stewed or diced tomatoes

1   can (6 ounces) tomato paste

2   cups V-8 juice

1   cup white wine

8   cups vegetable stock or water

3   teaspoons ground chili powder

2   teaspoons ground cumin

2   teaspoons ground coriander

1 1/2 teaspoons dried oregano

1 1/2 teaspoons dried basil

2   to 3 bay leaves
    Kosher salt, to taste

1   jalapeño or 1/2 habanero pepper, minced

1   tablespoon freshly squeezed lime juice

1   cup corn kernels, fresh or frozen

1   bunch scallions, diced

1/4 cup chopped fresh cilantro
    Freshly ground black pepper, to taste

155

■ Place the beans and chickpeas in a deep bowl. Add enough cold water to cover by two inches. Place the bowl in the refrigerator and soak the beans overnight. Drain before using.

■ Heat a stockpot over medium-high heat. Add the olive oil, garlic, onion, carrots, and bell peppers. Sauté for 7 minutes, stirring frequently. Add the drained beans and chickpeas, tomatoes, tomato paste, V-8 juice, wine, stock, chili powder, cumin, coriander, oregano, basil, bay leaves, and salt. Cover the pot and bring to a boil. Reduce the heat to medium and simmer for 1 1/2 hours, or until the beans are tender and fully cooked.

■ Remove from the heat and discard bay leaves. Add the jalapeño pepper, lime juice, corn, scallions, cilantro, pepper, and additional salt, to taste.

Makes 12 servings

Veal and Portobello Mushroom Stew

This special recipe breaks the bank, but it's worth every bite. It shows off the sweet, mellow flavor of tender, milk-fed veal. I make a batch at home on the weekends and then live off of it for a few days during the week. It can easily be dressed up or dressed down. I have served this stew to important company on my best china, and to my family in the dead of winter, when we all came to the table in pajamas and slippers. Whatever the occasion, it invariably tastes fabulous. For a nice presentation, spoon it over buttered pappardelle pasta, and then top with freshly grated Parmesan cheese and torn fresh basil leaves.

2 pounds veal stew meat, cut into bite-size pieces

2 cups flour seasoned with salt and pepper, to taste

4 tablespoons olive oil

1 large fennel bulb, diced into bite-size pieces

3 cloves garlic, minced

1 pound Italian cipollini onions, peeled

5 large portobello mushroom caps, diced into bite-sized pieces

3 cups Merlot

3 cups veal or chicken stock

2 cups (16 ounces) canned stewed tomatoes

1 cup (8 ounces) canned ground or crushed tomatoes

2 bay leaves

2 teaspoons dried oregano

2 teaspoons dried basil

1 teaspoon fennel seeds

1 tablespoon balsamic vinegar

Kosher salt and freshly ground black pepper, to taste

■ Dredge the veal pieces in the seasoned flour until coated on all sides. Shake off the excess flour. Heat a large Dutch oven or braising pan over medium-high heat and add the olive oil. Add the veal, a few pieces at a time, so the pan is not overcrowded. Cook, rotating the meat with tongs until brown and crispy on all sides. Place the browned veal on a large plate. Repeat until all the veal is browned. Set aside.

■ Preheat the oven to 325 degrees. To the same pan used for browning the veal, add the fennel, garlic, and onions. Sauté for 5 minutes, stirring frequently. Add the mushrooms and browned veal. Sauté an additional 2 minutes. Add the Merlot, stock, stewed and ground tomatoes, bay leaves, oregano, basil, and fennel seeds. Stir well. Cover the pot, place in the oven, and bake for 3 hours or until the veal is soft and tender. Remove from the oven, discard the bay leaves, and add the vinegar, salt, and pepper.

Makes 6 to 8 servings

Spring in a Bowl

Spring never comes soon enough in New England. By the end of February, after months of leafless trees, gray skies, and roadside piles of snow, we're all longing for something green. These soups take advantage of the first vegetables to reach the market—asparagus, spring onions, peas, and green beans. They are also loaded with fresh herbs including dill, basil, and mint. Many make a colorful, luscious first course for Easter or Passover meals. To follow the growing season, the recipes at the end of the chapter use early summer ingredients. Vegetarians will find plenty of options here, including our bestselling Eggplant, Roasted Red Pepper, and Mint soup.

To celebrate the arrival of spring in 1973, my third-grade teacher, Mrs. Joy Kant, announced that we were going to have a class brunch. From a cookie tin, she picked names of five children who could go to the grocery store and buy the food with her.

"I just have to be picked," I thought to myself. I sat at my desk with fingers crossed on both hands, crossed legs, and did I mention I was cross-eyed? I guess luck was with me, because I was the first name she announced!

I was so happy to stroll the aisles of the A&P with my favorite teacher. We bought pancake mix, maple syrup, butter, bacon, hot cocoa with marshmallows, and lots of orange juice. As we stood in line waiting to pay, I eyed all that was on the conveyer belt. I knew that something was missing. I tugged on Mrs. Kant's plaid Navy blue and gray skirt and told her we needed eggs. Who ever heard of a brunch without eggs? I was going to make my famous scrambled eggs for the class.

The day before the brunch, I started to pack up my little bag of tricks. I grabbed a few of my mother's whisks, forks, spatulas, and white Corelle mixing bowls. I also packed her large, beige electric frying pan, making sure to include the plug. In the refrigerator, I set aside butter, two dozen brown eggs, and light cream, then found the Kosher salt, and the *pièce de résistance*, Lawry's seasoned salt.

As I walked to school I begged my sister Janie to help me carry my frying pan, but she was so embarrassed that she walked ahead and pretended not to know me. I finally made it to class, and gratefully plopped everything down on my desk to start getting organized. Mrs. Kant told us that we were going to work in pairs. I did not want a partner, and emphasized the point by separating my desk from the girl who sat next to me. I told Mrs. Kant that I would like to work on my own, and suggested that the girl work with another group. To my relief, everyone agreed to this switch.

I made a sign for the front of my booth, and then I started making eggs to order for each kid in my class. When Mrs. Kant told me it was my turn to take a break and eat the food that my classmates had prepared, I told her that I needed to stay at my station and cook. All of the kids in the class were so impressed with how quickly I could make eggs that they all gave me a round of applause. It was my first catering job.

Lamb and Barley Soup with Mint

I call this shish kabob soup because it tastes as wonderful as a skewer of lamb and vegetables. I cook the meat until it is soft and tender, then add it to the soup.

Lamb

2 pounds boneless leg of lamb, cut into cubes
2¹/2 quarts (10 cups) water
¹/4 cup red wine vinegar
1 teaspoon kosher salt

Soup

3 tablespoons olive oil
4 cloves garlic, minced
1 large Spanish onion, peeled and diced
2 ribs celery, diced
4 carrots, peeled and diced or sliced
3 parsnips, peeled and diced or sliced

1 red bell pepper, seeded and diced
  Cooked lamb (from recipe)
1 cup pearl barley
1 cup (8 ounces) canned stewed tomatoes
8 cups beef or chicken stock
1 cup red wine
2 bay leaves
1 teaspoon dried oregano
  Juice and zest of 1 lemon
5 dashes Worcestershire sauce
1 bunch fresh mint leaves, chopped
  Kosher salt and freshly ground black pepper, to taste

For the lamb: In an 8 to 10-quart stockpot over high heat combine the lamb, water, vinegar, and salt. Bring to a boil. Reduce the heat to medium and simmer briskly for 1¹/2 hours. Drain and discard the cooking liquid. Set aside.

For the soup: Heat the olive oil in a stockpot over medium-high heat. Add the garlic, onion, celery, carrots, and parsnips and sauté for 10 minutes. Add the bell pepper and sauté an additional 3 minutes. Add the cooked lamb, barley, tomatoes, stock, red wine, bay leaves, and oregano. Bring to a boil and reduce the heat to medium and simmer for 45 to 50 minutes. Add the lemon juice and zest, Worcestershire sauce, mint, salt, and pepper and stir well. Remove and discard the bay leaves before serving.

Makes 12 servings

163

Sweet Green Pea Soup with Fresh Mint

This soup tastes as fresh as its bright green color. Around here, everyone is ready for a spoonful as soon as the crocuses poke up from the last of the snow. It's a relatively quick and easy recipe. The fresh mint added at the end gives the soup a clean finish. It makes a beautiful first course for Easter, as it goes really well with rack of lamb. The pale white, slightly tangy crème fraiche contrasts nicely with the soup's color and earthy flavor.

3 tablespoons salted butter	1/4 cup julienned fresh mint leaves, plus additional, for garnish
1 1/2 cups chopped spring onions or Spanish onions	1 cup heavy cream
1 bulb fennel or anise, diced	1 teaspoon Worcestershire sauce
2 whole cloves garlic, peeled	Kosher salt and freshly ground black pepper, to taste
2 Yukon Gold potatoes, peeled and diced small	Crème fraîche, for garnish
6 cups chicken stock	
2 packages (16 ounces each) frozen peas	

In a stockpot melt the butter over medium-high heat. Add the spring onions, fennel, garlic, and potatoes and sauté for 15 minutes. Add the stock and bring to a boil. Reduce the heat to medium, cover the pot, and cook until the potatoes are soft and tender, 30 to 35 minutes. Remove from the heat. Add the frozen peas and mint leaves. Puree the soup in the pot using a hand blender or working in batches with a regular blender until very smooth. Add the cream, Worcestershire sauce, salt, and pepper. Puree once again until completely blended. Return the soup to the stove and cook an additional 5 minutes. Garnish each serving with a dollop of crème fraîche and a pinch of mint leaves.

Makes 8 to 10 servings

Spring onions—the first of the season—will be a real treat if you can find them. Their green shoots look a bit like leeks, and their white bulbs are about the size of a golf ball. They are harvested young and have a bracingly strong flavor.

Asparagus, Potato, and Herb Soup

Asparagus is to spring what apples are to fall. Both unmistakably signal the change in season, though the effect is somewhat diminished now that they have become more available year-round.

2¹/2 pounds asparagus, washed and trimmed

3 tablespoons butter

3 whole cloves garlic, peeled

1 Spanish onion, peeled and diced

2 ribs celery, diced

1 bulb fennel, diced

6 medium Yukon Gold or red bliss potatoes, peeled and roughly chopped

6 cups vegetable or chicken stock

1 cup white wine

8 fresh basil leaves, chopped

6 sprigs fresh dill, chopped

¹/4 cup chopped fresh tarragon leaves

1 tablespoon dry mustard

2 cups light cream

Kosher salt and freshly ground black pepper, to taste

2 hard-boiled eggs, sliced for garnish

Cut off the asparagus tips and set aside. Using a food processor fitted with the slicer blade, cut the asparagus stems into small slices. This will help break up the fibrous threads that could make the soup stringy. Don't try to use a knife—it won't be effective for this job.

Melt the butter in a stockpot over medium-high heat. Add the garlic, onion, celery, and fennel. Sauté for 7 minutes. Add the sliced asparagus and potatoes. Sauté for an additional 3 minutes. Add the stock and wine. Bring to a boil. Reduce the heat to medium and simmer until the potatoes are soft and tender, 30 to 35 minutes.

Remove from the heat. Add the basil, dill, tarragon, mustard, cream, salt, and pepper. Puree the soup in the pot using a hand blender or working in batches with a regular blender until smooth.

Bring a small pot of water to a boil. Add the reserved asparagus tips and cook for 2 minutes. Drain and add the tips to the soup.

Makes 8 to 10 servings

Potato and Roasted Leek Soup

photo on page 160

Potato and leek soup is a culinary classic. This recipe gives it an update by roasting sliced leeks in the oven until they are soft and sweet. I like using Yukon Gold potatoes, as they have a nice, buttery color and flavor. March is the perfect time to make this soup because leeks are just coming into season.

7 pounds leeks, washed and sliced into 1/4–inch rounds (white and pale green parts only), divided

8 tablespoons salted butter, melted, divided

Kosher salt and freshly ground black pepper, to taste

4 whole cloves garlic, peeled

6 to 8 Yukon Gold potatoes, peeled and diced

8 cups chicken stock or broth

1 teaspoon ground bay leaves

1 teaspoon celery salt

1 teaspoon crushed red pepper flakes

1 tablespoon Worcestershire sauce

1/2 teaspoon ground nutmeg

1 1/2 cups light cream

Snipped fresh chives, for garnish

Preheat the oven to 375 degrees. Place 2 pounds (about 4 cups) of the sliced leeks into a roasting pan. Drizzle with 2 tablespoons of the melted butter and season with salt and pepper. Place in the oven and roast for 25 to 30 minutes, stirring halfway through cooking to keep the leeks from burning and sticking to the bottom of the pan. Remove from the oven and set aside.

In a large stockpot add the remaining 6 tablespoons of butter, the remaining 5 pounds of leeks, and the garlic. Sauté over medium-high heat for 15 minutes, or until the leeks are caramelized. Add the potatoes and sauté an additional 5 minutes. Add the stock, cover the pot, and bring to a boil. Reduce the heat to medium and simmer until the potatoes are soft and tender, 30 to 35 minutes.

Remove the pot from the heat and add the bay leaves, celery salt, red pepper flakes, Worcestershire sauce, and nutmeg. Puree the soup in the pot using a hand blender or working in batches with a regular blender until smooth. Add the light cream and salt and pepper, to taste. Puree once again until the cream is thoroughly incorporated. Reserve a few roasted leeks, for garnish, and stir the remaining roasted leeks into the soup until they are evenly distributed. Garnish with roasted leeks and freshly snipped chives.

Makes 8 to 10 servings

In Boston, sometimes called America's most Irish city (about 15 percent of the city's residents have ancestors from Ireland), this soup has always been a customer favorite around St. Patrick's Day. Play up the theme by serving it in an emerald-hued bowl, sprinkled with chives and lots of roasted leeks.

Minestrone Verde

The word verde means green in Italian, and green vegetables—with just a few beans for texture and protein—are the theme of this Italian-inspired minestrone soup. Use your imagination when making this soup, and snap up the green vegetables that look crisp and fresh—wherever you do your shopping.

3 tablespoons olive oil	4 zucchini, diced into 1/2-inch chunks
4 cloves garlic, minced	1/2 pound okra, fresh or frozen, sliced
1 large Spanish onion, peeled and diced	1/2 pound frozen fava or lima beans
2 ribs celery, sliced	1 can (16 ounces) white cannellini beans, drained and rinsed
2 parsnips, peeled and sliced	
4 carrots, preferably Sunshine, peeled and sliced	1/2 pound fresh spinach leaves
16 cups vegetable or chicken stock	1 cup frozen peas
2 bay leaves	1 tablespoon balsamic vinegar
2 teaspoons dried oregano	1 bunch fresh basil leaves, chopped
1/2 pound fresh green beans or Roma beans, tough ends removed	2 tablespoons extra-virgin olive oil
	Kosher salt and freshly ground black pepper, to taste

Heat a stockpot over medium-high heat. Add the olive oil, garlic, onion, celery, parsnips, and carrots. Sauté for 10 minutes. Add the stock, bay leaves, and oregano and bring to a boil. Reduce the heat to medium and simmer for 12 minutes. Add the green beans, zucchini, and okra. Simmer an additional 7 minutes. Add the fava beans, cannellini beans, spinach, and frozen peas and stir to wilt the spinach. Add the vinegar, basil, olive oil, salt, and pepper and simmer an additional 3 to 5 minutes. Remove and discard the bay leaves before serving.

Makes 16 servings

Carrot and Ginger Soup

Those pre-washed, bite-sized carrots at the supermarket have made this vegetable a lot more convenient to grab for a snack. Still, the crunchy, raw sticks can't match the appeal of carrots in a soup. When cooked, carrots add texture, body—and a pretty, orange glow. They also contain lots of Vitamin A. In this recipe, honey enhances their natural sweetness. Fresh ginger root adds a contrasting note of heat and spice. The overall flavor profile is similar to pumpkin pie. When I serve it at home, I like to garnish the top with a few pieces of candied ginger, and drizzle it with a bit of honey.

3 tablespoons butter	8 cups chicken or vegetable stock
2 whole cloves garlic, peeled	1 teaspoon ground coriander
1 large Spanish onion, peeled and diced	1 teaspoon ground ginger
2 ribs celery, sliced	1/2 cup honey
3 pounds carrots, peeled and sliced	11/2 cups heavy cream
3 tablespoons peeled and chopped fresh ginger	Kosher salt and freshly ground black pepper, to taste

In a large, heavy-bottomed stockpot over medium-high heat, melt the butter. Add the garlic, onion, celery, carrots, and gingerroot. Sauté for 10 minutes, stirring frequently. Pour the stock over the vegetables and bring to a boil. Lower the heat slightly and simmer until the carrots are soft and tender, 30 to 35 minutes.

Remove from the heat. Add the coriander, ground ginger, and honey. Puree the soup in the pot using a hand blender or working in batches with a regular blender until smooth. Add the heavy cream and season with salt and pepper. Stir until the ingredients are well combined.

Makes 8 to 10 servings

This soup fits in nicely with an Easter or Passover menu. For Easter, it goes well with rack of lamb, roast ham, or almost anything you could imagine serving for the holiday. For Passover, it works well with classic, oven-roasted chicken.

Eggplant, Roasted Red Pepper, and Mint Soup

Roasted eggplant is probably most familiar to people as the key ingredient in the Middle Eastern spread, baba ghanoush. I knew that eggplant would make a great base for a soup if I could somehow get beyond its unappealing gray color. I found the solution by adding roasted red peppers and tomatoes. I also added mint to contrast with the concentrated, almost smoky flavors of the pepper and eggplant. The color turned into a beautiful, creamy coral, and the soup has become one of our most popular vegetarian selections.

For a Middle Eastern touch, serve the soup with Homemade Toasted Pita Chips (see Syrian Chickpea Soup on page 106).

3 whole, medium-sized eggplant	2 cups tomato juice
3 tablespoons butter	2 cups light cream
4 whole cloves garlic, peeled	1 bunch fresh mint leaves, washed
1 large Spanish onion, peeled and diced	5 dashes Tabasco sauce
2 ribs celery, sliced	5 dashes Worcestershire sauce
5 carrots, peeled and sliced	Kosher salt and freshly ground black pepper, to taste
4 cups roasted red peppers	
6 cups vegetable or chicken stock	

Preheat the oven to 400 degrees. With a fork, prick each eggplant in several places. Place the eggplants in a roasting pan and bake for 30 to 35 minutes. Remove from the oven and let cool. With a small knife, slice each eggplant open lengthwise and remove the pulp. Set aside the pulp and discard the skins.

In a stockpot melt the butter over medium-high heat. Add the garlic, onion, celery, and carrots. Sauté for 10 minutes. Add the eggplant pulp, roasted red peppers, stock, and tomato juice. Bring to a boil. Reduce the heat to medium and simmer for 35 minutes. Remove from the heat and add the cream, mint leaves, Tabasco sauce, and Worcestershire sauce. Season with salt and pepper. Puree the soup in the pot using a hand blender or working in batches with a regular blender until very smooth. Place the pot back on the stove and simmer an additional 5 to 8 minutes.

Makes 10 to 12 servings

When you are removing the eggplant pulp from its skin, wear rubber gloves, as the juices can trigger an allergic reaction that causes itching.

Black Bean, Habanero Chile, and Yellow Rice Soup

My husband, Paul, and I visit Captiva Island, Florida, as often as we can, not only to escape the dreary New England winter, but also because it's the place we first met as interns in a chef training program. We always rent a boat for the day because that's the only way we can get to our favorite restaurant, Barnacle Phil's. The tables are in little huts on the beach, and we don't have to wear shoes. Even the servers go barefoot. The specialty is black beans with yellow rice, served in a big bowl with freshly chopped onions on top and Tabasco sauce on the side. This dish is the main reason we keep coming back.

I tried to capture all the flavors of Barnacle Phil's beans in this soup. Every time I make it, I remember—if only fleetingly—our great barefoot escape. The habanero chile pepper, a Caribbean favorite, is super hot, so you only need one for the entire soup. See the tip on page 73 for instructions on handling hot peppers.

Yellow rice

- 2 tablespoons olive oil
- 1/2 cup chopped onion
- 1 cup jasmine rice
- 2 cups water
- 2 teaspoons kosher salt
  Pinch of saffron or turmeric

Soup

- 1 pound dried black beans
- 3 tablespoons olive oil
- 4 cloves garlic, minced
- 1 large Spanish onion, peeled and diced

- 2 ribs celery, diced
- 2 1/2 quarts (10 cups) vegetable or chicken stock
- 4 cups (32 ounces) canned crushed tomatoes
- 2 teaspoons ground coriander
- 1 cup sherry
- 1/4 cup chopped fresh cilantro
  Kosher salt and freshly ground black pepper, to taste
- 1 habanero pepper, seeded and minced
- 1 tablespoon lime juice
  Cooked yellow rice (from recipe)
- 1 bunch scallions, chopped, for garnish

For the yellow rice: Heat a 3-quart saucepan over medium-high heat and add the olive oil. Add the onion and sauté for 5 minutes, or until a pale golden color. Add the rice and continue to sauté for 3 minutes more. Add the water, salt, and saffron. Bring to a boil, cover the pan, and reduce the heat to low. Cook for 15 to 20 minutes, or until all the water is absorbed and the rice is fluffy.

For the soup: Place the beans in a deep bowl and add water to cover by 2 inches. Place in the refrigerator and soak overnight. Drain before using.

Heat a stockpot over medium-high heat. Add the olive oil, garlic, onion, and celery. Sauté, stirring frequently, for 10 minutes. Add the beans, stock, tomatoes, coriander, and sherry. Bring to a boil. Reduce the heat to medium. Simmer for 1 1/4 hours, or until the beans are tender. Add the cilantro and season with salt and pepper. Add the habanero pepper, lime juice, and rice. Garnish with the scallions.

Makes 10 to 12 servings

ⓥ Spinach and Zucchini Bisque with Roasted Leeks

I started making this soup one summer when a customer brought us the zucchini that seemed to be inundating her garden. Some of them were so big they would not even fit into the pot. (We used those whoppers for decorations—guaranteed to give customers a laugh). The rest went into the first batches of this spinach and zucchini bisque. Our lawyer, Nina, is always glad when it goes on the menu because it's one of the few ways she can get her children to eat some vegetables. Now this is one of our longest-running spring and summer soups.

Roasted Leeks

- 4 leeks, thoroughly washed and sliced about 1 inch thick
- 2 tablespoons olive oil
  Kosher salt and freshly ground black pepper, to taste

Soup

- 3 tablespoons butter
- 3 whole cloves garlic, peeled
- 1 Spanish onion, peeled and diced
- 3 ribs celery, diced
- 1 bulb fennel, diced
- 2 pounds zucchini, cut into chunks
- 3 Yukon Gold potatoes, peeled and cut into chunks
- 8 cups vegetable stock
- 1/2 teaspoon ground nutmeg
- 1 pound fresh spinach leaves
- 2 cups light cream
  Kosher salt and freshly ground black pepper, to taste
  Roasted leeks (from recipe)

For the roasted leeks: Preheat the oven to 425 degrees. In a mixing bowl toss the leeks with the olive oil and season with salt and pepper. Place in a roasting pan and bake for 20 to 25 minutes, tossing occasionally with a spoon so they brown on all sides.

For the soup: Melt the butter in a stockpot over medium-high heat. Add the garlic, onion, celery, and fennel. Sauté for 5 minutes. Add the zucchini, potatoes, and stock. Bring to a boil. Reduce the heat to medium and simmer until the potatoes are soft and tender, 30 to 35 minutes. Remove from the heat. Add the nutmeg and spinach leaves, stirring until the spinach wilts.

Puree the soup in the pot using a hand blender or working in batches with a regular blender until smooth. Add the cream. Season with salt and pepper. Stir in the roasted leeks.

Makes 8 servings

Summer Soothers

Hot and humid days can sap your strength, keeping you just as housebound as you are in the winter. These chilled soups bring cold comfort when you want something more substantial than an ice cream cone. For an appetizer, cucumber makes a cool base to be mixed with yogurt and chives, or avocado and lime. You can serve raspberry-nectarine gazpacho at a picnic, or a seafood variation of the recipe for dinner. Fruit works beautifully in dessert soups, ending any meal with a pureed burst of sweetness. Most of these soups are vegetarian.

I always knew my husband, Paul, was a kindhearted person, but one scorching June day, he did something so nice that it brought me to tears. As he was turning the corner on his way into work that day, a homeless man approached him. Paul had seen him around the neighborhood, but hadn't really said more than hello. On this day, he stopped Paul, looked into his eyes, and said, "I don't feel very well today. I am just not doing well. I feel sick and need some food." His eyes were glazed. Paul told him that he would be right back. He went into our store and grabbed some pints of soup. He placed them in a bag with fresh rolls, cookies, and a beverage, then went back outside and found the man. Pointing out a shady spot, Paul told him to sit down and eat so that he would feel better. I never thought our soup could offer such sustenance on a hot summer day, and I was grateful to Paul for giving it away to someone who truly needed it.

⊙ Cucumber, Avocado, and Lime Soup

This is one of the first cold soups we ever started making in our stores. Avocadoes sometimes get a bad name because they are high in fat, but they contain no cholesterol and are a good source of fiber and Vitamin C. We have found that anything containing avocado is a huge seller because of the smooth and creamy texture. In this recipe, the freshly squeezed lime juice and fresh cilantro intensify the avocado's slightly nutty flavor. Cucumbers add a cool crunch that makes this soup so refreshing.

10	ripe avocados, peeled and quartered	6	cups vegetable or chicken stock
2	English cucumbers, peeled and diced, divided	2	cups light cream
1	bunch scallions, diced, divided	2	tablespoons chopped fresh cilantro
2	tablespoons extra-virgin olive oil	4	dashes Tabasco sauce
	Juice of 3 limes		Kosher salt and freshly ground black pepper, to taste
	Zest of 2 limes		

■ Place the avocados in a 6 to 8-quart bowl or stockpot. Add half the cucumbers and half the scallions. Add the olive oil, lime juice, lime zest, stock, cream, cilantro, Tabasco sauce, salt, and pepper.

■ Puree the soup in the pot using a hand blender or working in batches with a regular blender until smooth and creamy. Stir in the remaining cucumbers and scallions. Chill in the refrigerator for at least 3 hours.

Makes 10 to 12 servings

Chilled English Cucumber and Chive Soup with Greek Yogurt

This pretty, light green soup contrasts sweet cucumber with tart yogurt and lemon juice. The thick texture of Greek yogurt works particularly well with the other ingredients. If you can't find it at a supermarket, substitute plain, whole milk yogurt or sour cream. This is good for a ladies' luncheon on a hot day. The soup would be hopelessly bland without sweet onions, pickles, and chives perking up each bite. It is best to prepare it the day you serve it so the vegetables stay fresh and crunchy.

4 English cucumbers, divided	1 pint plain Greek yogurt
1 Vidalia onion, peeled and minced	1 cup light cream
2 half-sour pickles, diced	2 cups vegetable or chicken stock
3 cloves garlic, minced	2 teaspoons ground coriander
Juice of 2 lemons	2 teaspoons onion powder
1 tablespoon extra-virgin olive oil	1/2 teaspoon Tabasco sauce
Kosher salt and freshly ground black pepper, to taste	2 bunches fresh chives, minced

■ Peel and dice 3 of the cucumbers. Using a sharp knife or a mandoline, cut 16 paper-thin slices from the remaining cucumber. Set aside. Peel and dice the rest of the cucumber. In a 4 to 6-quart glass bowl place the diced cucumbers, onion, pickles, and garlic. Squeeze the lemon juice over the vegetables. Add the olive oil, salt, and pepper.

■ In a separate bowl combine the yogurt, cream, stock, coriander, onion powder, Tabasco sauce, and chives. Stir to combine thoroughly and pour over the vegetables. Season with salt and pepper, if necessary. Cover the bowl and refrigerate for at least 1 hour. Serve in chilled bowls with the thin slices of cucumber on top.

Makes 6 to 8 servings

A mandoline, a special kitchen tool made from a flat base with adjustable blades on top, is primarily used for slicing firm fruits and vegetables into uniform shapes (such as julienne and waffle cuts). It is particularly useful for creating paper-thin slices of ingredients, including the cucumbers used in this recipe.

Seafood Gazpacho

Gazpacho, a soup designed to be served cold, originated in the Andalusian region of southern Spain, where it helped mitigate the scorching climate. The basic recipe combines tomatoes, bell peppers, and cucumbers with bread crumbs and seasonings. In this variation, I add clam juice and fresh seafood to take advantage of the summer catch.

3	cups bottled clam juice, divided
1/2	pound scallops
1/4	pound shrimp
1	English cucumber, peeled and diced
1	cup diced red bell pepper
1	cup diced yellow bell pepper
1	cup diced ripe tomatoes
1/2	cup diced Vidalia onion
2	cloves garlic, minced
3/4	cup extra-virgin olive oil

	Juice of 3 limes
	Kosher salt and freshly ground black pepper, to taste
1	tablespoon sherry vinegar
1	can (46 ounces) V-8 juice
2	tablespoons chopped fresh cilantro
2	tablespoons chopped fresh basil
1	avocado, peeled and diced
8	ounces fresh crabmeat
1/2	teaspoon Tabasco sauce

■ In a 2-quart stockpot place 2 cups of the clam juice, the scallops, and shrimp over high heat. Bring to a boil. Reduce the heat to medium-high and simmer for 5 to 6 minutes. Drain and set aside. If not using immediately, chill in the refrigerator until ready to use.

■ In a large bowl, combine the cucumber, red and yellow peppers, tomatoes, and onion. Add the garlic, olive oil, lime juice, salt, and pepper. Refrigerate for 30 minutes. Add the vinegar, V-8 juice, the remaining 1 cup clam juice, cilantro, basil, avocado, crabmeat, and Tabasco sauce. Stir well. Add the cooked scallops and shrimp. Season with salt and pepper, to taste. Cover the bowl and chill in the refrigerator for at least 4 hours.

Makes 10 servings

Late Summer Raspberry-Nectarine Gazpacho

photo on page 178

This recipe tries to preserve the traits of a traditional gazpacho while adding the intoxicating fruit flavors of raspberries and nectarines. For a picnic on a hot summer day, I like to pack the thoroughly chilled soup into pint glass Mason jars and put them in my cooler. I am always so eager to eat that by 10 a.m., I start asking my husband, Paul, every ten minutes if it's almost time for lunch yet. Usually, by 11:30, he gives in and I get to twist open the lids. Ahh, euphoria!

4	cups red raspberries
6	nectarines, peeled and diced
1	bunch scallions, thinly sliced
1	yellow bell pepper, seeded and diced small
1	orange bell pepper, seeded and diced small
1	long English cucumber, diced small
2	ripe tomatoes, finely diced
3	cloves garlic, minced
1/4	cup extra-virgin olive oil
2	tablespoons raspberry vinegar

6	cups V-8 Splash juice (or any fruity juice blend)
	Pulp from 1 passion fruit (optional)
6	cups tomato juice
1	cup fresh bread crumbs
	Juice of 2 fresh limes
1/2	bunch fresh cilantro, chopped
1/2	teaspoon green Tabasco sauce
	Kosher salt and freshly ground black pepper, to taste

■ In a very large and deep bowl, combine the raspberries, nectarines, scallions, yellow and orange peppers, cucumber, tomatoes, garlic, olive oil, vinegar, V-8 Splash, passion fruit if using, tomato juice, bread crumbs, lime juice, cilantro, Tabasco sauce, salt, and pepper and stir well.

■ Pour 1 quart of the soup into a blender. Puree until the texture is mostly smooth, but a few chunks remain. Return to the bowl and stir to incorporate. Cover the bowl and refrigerate for at least 3 to 4 hours before serving.

■ For a dramatic presentation, ladle the soup into chilled large red wine goblets. Top with fresh raspberries and a slice or two of freshly cut nectarine.

Makes 8 to 10 servings

Chilled Beet and Raspberry Soup

You can't get any more vibrant than this magenta soup, which pairs earthy beets with sweet, delicate raspberries. I think it's a toss-up whether the flavor or the color is more appealing. Garnish each serving with sprigs of fresh dill and whole raspberries. Serve it with Farmers' Market Salad (see page 222) for a refreshing lunch during one of summer's hottest days.

3   pounds beets

3   tablespoons butter

2   cloves garlic, minced

1   cup chopped Spanish onions

2   ribs celery, diced

6   cups chicken or vegetable stock

1   pint fresh raspberries

2   cups light cream

2   tablespoons chopped fresh dill

1   tablespoon raspberry vinegar

    Kosher salt and freshly-ground black pepper, to taste

■ Wash and trim the stems from the beets. Place in a 4-quart pot. Add 3 quarts of water and bring to a boil over high heat. Reduce the heat to medium and simmer, uncovered, for 40 minutes or until the beets are tender when pierced with a knife. Drain and place under cold running water. Peel off the skins and cut into large chunks. Set aside.

■ Melt the butter in a stockpot over medium-high heat. Add the garlic, onions, celery, and beets. Sauté for 5 to 7 minutes, stirring frequently. Add the chicken stock and bring to a boil. Reduce the heat to medium and simmer for 30 minutes.

■ Remove from the stove and add the raspberries. Puree the soup in the pot using a hand blender or working in batches with a regular blender until smooth. Strain through a sieve or fine mesh strainer to remove any raspberry seeds. Add the cream, dill, vinegar, salt and pepper. Puree once more until thoroughly blended. Let cool at room temperature for 1 hour. Refrigerate at least 3 hours before serving.

Makes 6 to 8 servings

187

ⓥ Mango and Lime Soup with Crème Fraîche

The intoxicating flavor and aroma of mangoes is probably what makes this our most popular fruit soup. One bite is simultaneously thick, creamy, and refreshing. I think of it as our sexiest soup. The flavor really depends on ripe mangoes, which should have yellowish-red skin and flesh that is soft but not mushy when you lightly press the outside with your finger. Buy them a few days in advance, when their skin is still slightly green, to make sure they are ripe when you make the soup.

10 mangoes, peeled and cut into chunks	1/8 teaspoon salt
2 cups apricot nectar	1 cup light cream
3/4 cup white wine	1 cup crème fraîche
1/4 cup packed brown sugar	Fresh mint leaves, for garnish
Juice and zest of 2 limes	

■ Place the mangoes in a 4 to 6-quart pot. Add the apricot nectar, wine, and brown sugar. Bring to a boil over medium-high heat. Lower the heat to medium and simmer for 20 minutes. Remove from the heat and add the lime juice, lime zest, and salt. Add the light cream and crème fraîche.

■ Puree the soup in the pot using a hand blender or working in batches with a regular blender until smooth. Place the soup in a glass or plastic container and refrigerate for at least 5 hours before serving. Garnish with mint leaves.

Makes 8 to 10 servings

Crème fraîche is a French-style thickened cream that with a slightly tangy flavor similar to sour cream. It can be found in good cheese shops or in the cheese section of the grocery store. It also works well in hot soups, as it does not break apart when heated.

Ⓥ Hungarian Bing Cherry Soup

This versatile soup's scarlet hue is always a conversation piece. Garnish each serving with a dollop of sour cream or crème fraiche to offset the color. Served hot, the soup makes a good first course for an entrée of duck or veal. It can also be served cold, presented in a glass serving bowl, or ladled into chilled red wine goblets. Garnish with fresh cherries with the stems still attached.

3 cans (16 ounces each) dark, sweet cherries, drained, divided	1/4 teaspoon ground cinnamon
2 cups apple juice	1 teaspoon raspberry vinegar
2 cups Burgundy wine	1 teaspoon kosher salt
3/4 cup packed light brown sugar	1 cup light cream
Juice of 1 lemon	3 heaping tablespoons sour cream
1/4 teaspoon ground ginger	2 tablespoons Kirsch liqueur

■ In a stockpot over medium-high heat add 2 cans of the cherries, the apple juice, wine, brown sugar, lemon juice, ginger, cinnamon, vinegar, and salt. Bring to a boil. Reduce the heat to medium and simmer for 10 to 15 minutes.

■ Remove from the heat and add the cream, sour cream, and Kirsch. Puree the soup in the pot using a hand blender or working in batches with a regular blender until smooth and creamy. Pour the soup into a large serving bowl and add the remaining 1 can cherries. Stir to combine. If serving cold, chill at least 5 to 6 hours before serving.

Makes 8 to 10 servings

Our chocolate variation of this soup has become a dessert sensation. It started out as an experiment one day when my sous chef and baker, Steve Luca—a serious chocolate freak—sprinkled some cocoa powder into a small batch. Needless to say, the combination was a keeper. To make it, add 1/4 cup of cocoa powder to the recipe right after the brown sugar. I can always count on my staff to come up with great ideas like this one.

ⓥ Honey-Apricot Soup

photo on
page 178

When my husband, Paul, and I were newly married, we rented part of a two-family home. The soil was the most fertile I had ever seen—maybe because our landlord's name was Basil. We planted and grew all of our own vegetables. A spectacular apricot tree supplied us with fresh fruit all summer. When we grew tired of eating plain apricots, I made this soup. It's both tart and sweet, with a hint of ginger and a refreshingly silky texture. I like to serve it on a hot day, when you need a burst of sweetness and energy.

3 pounds ripe apricots	1/2 cup honey
3 cups apricot nectar	1/2 cup packed dark brown sugar
1 cup white wine	1/4 teaspoon salt
1 teaspoon ground ginger	1 cup light cream
Pinch of saffron threads	Honey, for garnish

■ Bring a 4-quart pot of water to boil over high heat. With a paring knife mark an X on the bottom of each apricot. Drop about four apricots at a time into the water and blanch for 30 seconds. Remove with a slotted spoon and immediately hold them under cold, running water. Gently remove the skins with your fingers. Cut in half and remove the pits. Slice 1 apricot, for garnish.

■ In a 4 to 6-quart pot over medium-high heat place the peeled apricot halves, apricot nectar, wine, ginger, and saffron. Bring to a boil. Reduce the heat to medium and simmer gently for 30 minutes.

■ Remove from the heat and add the honey, brown sugar, salt, and cream. Puree the soup in the pot using a hand blender or working in batches with a regular blender until smooth. Garnish each serving with an apricot slice and a drizzle of honey.

Makes 8 to 10 servings

Wild Maine Blueberry Soup

When my sister, Janie, was first married, she and her husband, Robby, bought a home in Kittery Point, Maine. My favorite part of the house was the blueberry bushes that surrounded their yard. In mid-July, what a delight it was waking up for Sunday brunch and going outside to gather blueberries for pancakes. I wanted to capture that experience when I created this soup. It simmers fresh blueberries with fruit juice and wine, then purees them with sour cream and brown sugar. Maine blueberries are smaller and more tart than the cultivated kind, but either one will work in this recipe.

3 pints fresh blueberries, divided

4 cups cranberry-blueberry juice blend or plain cranberry juice

3/4 cup white wine

Juice and zest of 1 orange

1/2 teaspoon ground cinnamon

1/2 cup packed dark brown sugar

1 pint sour cream

1/4 teaspoon salt

■ In a 4 to 6-quart soup pot place 2 1/2 pints of the blueberries. Add the juice blend, wine, orange juice and zest, cinnamon, and brown sugar. Bring to a boil over medium-high heat. Reduce the heat to medium and simmer for 12 to 15 minutes.

■ Remove from the heat and puree the soup in the pot using a hand blender or working in batches with a regular blender until the ingredients are mixed. With the blender running, add the sour cream, 1 cup at a time, and puree until smooth. Season with the salt. Stir in the remaining 1/2 pint blueberries. Refrigerate for at least 4 hours before serving.

Makes 8 to 10 servings

The purple color of this soup is especially vivid, making it quite a hit with kids who also go for outlandishly-hued breakfast cereals and sports drinks. Show it off by serving it in glass bowls.

Roasted Peach and Brown Sugar Soup

White peaches are some of my favorites, as each bite tastes like a great fruity wine. However, I use several different varieties of peaches for this soup so their flavors can blend. It tastes like a luscious peach cobbler.

12	cups water
12	ripe, assorted peaches
2	tablespoons melted butter
1 1/4	cups packed brown sugar
6	cups peach nectar
1	cup white wine
1	teaspoon ground ginger
1/4	teaspoon kosher salt
1	teaspoon fruit-flavored vinegar (such as raspberry)
2	cups light cream

■ In a 4 to 6-quart pot bring the water to a boil. With a paring knife, mark an X across the bottom of each peach. Drop the peaches two at a time into the boiling water. Blanch for 1 minute and remove with a slotted spoon. Place under cold, running water and remove the skins with your hands. Cut each peach in half and remove the pit. Continue until all the peaches are blanched, peeled, and pitted. Slice the peaches.

■ Preheat the oven to 425 degrees. Place the sliced peaches in a roasting pan. Add the butter and brown sugar and stir well to coat the peaches. Bake for 25 minutes.

■ In a stockpot over medium-high heat combine the roasted peaches, peach nectar, wine, ginger, salt, and vinegar. Bring to a boil. Reduce the heat to medium and simmer for 20 minutes.

■ Remove from the heat and puree the soup in the pot using a hand blender or working in batches with a regular blender until smooth. Stir in the cream. Place in a chilled bowl and refrigerate for at least 6 hours before serving.

Makes 8 to 10 servings

Since the flavor of this soup truly depends on ripe fruit, don't bother to make it unless peaches are in season.

Sumptuous Sandwiches

A bowl of soup can certainly be a meal in itself, but a sandwich makes a more interesting—and filling—accompaniment than a plain slice of bread. Some combinations, such as tomato soup and grilled cheese, work so well together it's hard to imagine one without the other. Other soups and sandwiches can be wildly mixed and matched to break up menu monotony. We have always served sandwiches at the New England Soup Factory, even though our focus is soup. If someone orders a sandwich and skips the soup, it's fine with us. Most of these recipes are variations on classics: Ham and cheese, tuna salad, and lobster rolls. There's also room for fun with selections like the Fallwich, which puts a Thanksgiving dinner between two slices of bread.

After Paul and I finished our culinary internship on Captiva Island in Florida, we were driving back to West Palm Beach to catch our plane to Boston. It was a long drive, and by the time we reached the city, I was ravenous. It was dark outside and I was looking for a place to eat. All of a sudden, in bright neon lights, I spotted a sign for Wolf's Delicatessen. I told Paul to pull over immediately! I hadn't eaten any Jewish food in three months, and I was dying for it. All I could think about was a pastrami sandwich with pickles and potato salad. Paul was flabbergasted that I would make such a big deal about a sandwich. Apparently, he had never tried a real delicatessen sandwich. I was about to introduce him. After two bites, Paul understood why I was so crazed. Now he craves deli sandwiches as much as I do. Whether we go to Manhattan, Miami, or Detroit, that's the only thing he wants. I know he has this hidden desire to open his own delicatessen, but I think that's just because he wants an excuse to eat pastrami sandwiches every day.

Roasted Vegetable Roll-Up in Whole Wheat Lavash

We are always trying to create new and interesting sandwiches for our vegetarian customers. Roasting really enhances the flavor of the vegetables in this one. When served warm, the mix of zucchini, summer squash, and bell peppers makes a nice change from lettuce and tomatoes. These sandwiches are great for lunch on the go, as they are easy to handle and eat.

1   large zucchini, diced into 1-inch chunks

1   large summer squash, diced into 1-inch chunks

1   red bell pepper, seeded and cut into large chunks

1   yellow bell pepper, seeded and cut into large chunks

1   red onion, peeled and cut into large chunks

2   carrots, peeled and sliced into 1-inch rounds

2   cloves garlic, minced

4   tablespoons olive oil

    Kosher salt and freshly ground black pepper, to taste

    Juice of 1 lemon

4   pieces whole wheat lavash

2   tablespoons chopped fresh basil

2   cups fresh spinach leaves

1/2 cup crumbled feta cheese, preferably French

Preheat the oven to 425 degrees. In a roasting pan place the zucchini, squash, red and yellow peppers, onion, carrots, garlic, and olive oil. Season with salt and pepper. Toss to coat the vegetables with the oil. Bake for 25 minutes, stirring occasionally. Remove from the oven and place the vegetables in a mixing bowl. Squeeze the lemon juice over the top and stir well.

Place the lavash on a cutting board. Cover each piece with a sprinkling of fresh basil and spinach leaves. Add the roasted vegetables and sprinkle with cheese. Season with salt and pepper. Starting at one end, roll up the sandwich onto itself like a jelly roll. Let rest for a minute, then slice each sandwich in half.

Makes 4 sandwiches

Lavash is a flat, round Armenian-style bread that looks a bit like pita bread without the pocket. Its shape makes it an ideal base for rolled sandwiches. It can be found at the grocery store or a Middle Eastern market.

Terrific Tuna Salad Sandwiches

Even when we offer several choices of sandwiches, tuna salad is always a bestseller. People can't seem to get enough of this classic. Our version starts with the basics—tuna (we use white albacore, but chunk light works just as well), celery, and just a little mayonnaise. For just a touch of sweetness with an added crunch, we stir in pickle relish or red pepper relish. On top go butter pickles for a distinctive finishing touch.

1   can (12 ounces) tuna,
    drained and squeezed dry

1   rib celery, diced small

2   tablespoons minced red onion

1   tablespoon pickle or red pepper relish
    Juice of 1/2 lemon

2   tablespoons mayonnaise

Kosher salt and freshly ground black
pepper, to taste

8   slices farmhouse white bread, toasted

1   cup lettuce leaves

8   tomato slices

16 bread and butter pickle slices

■ Place the tuna in a small mixing bowl. Gently mash with a fork to break into small pieces. Add the celery, onion, relish, and lemon juice. Toss together. Add the mayonnaise, salt, and pepper. Stir gently to combine.

■ Top 4 slices of the bread with the lettuce and 2 tomato slices. Season with salt and pepper. Spread a portion of the tuna salad over the tomatoes. Top with 4 slices of sweet pickles and the remaining slices of bread.

Makes 4 sandwiches

Turkey Avocado Club Sandwiches

This sandwich has deli roots with an added touch of California. It's tall and fat, and filled with layers of colorful lettuce, tomato, bacon, and onion. It's even better when you can find a local bakery that makes fresh marble rye bread with seeds. The homemade Russian dressing adds just the right tangy accent. This was one of the first sandwiches we ever served in the store, and it has become quite popular, to say the least.

Homemade Russian Dressing

- 1 cup mayonnaise
- 1/4 cup ketchup or chili sauce
- 1 tablespoon pickle relish
- 4 dashes Worcestershire sauce
- 1/4 teaspoon salt
- Freshly ground black pepper, to taste

Sandwiches

- 8 slices marble rye bread
- 6 to 8 tablespoons of homemade Russian dressing (from recipe)
- 4 to 6 pieces leafy green lettuce
- 8 slices tomato
- 4 slices red onion
- 1 pound roasted turkey breast, sliced thin
- 8 slices crisp-cooked bacon
- 16 slices ripe avocado
- Kosher salt and freshly ground black pepper, to taste

For the homemade Russian dressing: In a small bowl whisk together the mayonnaise, ketchup, relish, Worcestershire sauce, salt, and pepper. Continue whisking until well blended. Refrigerate until ready to use.

For the sandwiches: Spread the Russian dressing on each slice of bread. On 4 slices of the bread layer the lettuce, tomato, onion, turkey, 2 bacon slices, 4 avocado slices, salt, and pepper. Place the remaining 4 slices of bread on top and secure each sandwich with a toothpick. Slice in half or quarters.

Makes 4 sandwiches

Roast Beef Sandwiches with Garlic-Herb Spread

These café-style sandwiches, a variation on roast beef and Boursin, are easy to make at home, and travel well in lunchboxes or picnic baskets. Just don't skimp on the ingredients. Find a good-quality baguette with some crust; the bad ones are so flimsy that they flop back and forth when you pick them up! Purchase tender roast beef from a deli and ask that it be thinly sliced.

Garlic-Herb Spread

8 tablespoons butter, at room temperature

1 pound cream cheese, at room temperature

1/2 cup sour cream

2 tablespoons chopped fresh parsley

2 cloves garlic, minced

2 teaspoons dried oregano

2 teaspoons dried basil

1/2 teaspoon ground cumin

1/2 teaspoon dried thyme

Juice of 1 lemon

2 1/2 teaspoons kosher salt

1 1/2 teaspoons freshly ground black pepper

Sandwiches

1 large, crusty French baguette

6 tablespoons garlic-herb spread (from recipe)

4 to 6 large romaine lettuce leaves, washed and dried

1 large tomato, sliced

3/4 pound sliced roast beef

6 to 8 cornichons, sliced

Kosher salt and freshly ground black pepper, to taste

For the garlic-herb spread: Place the butter and cream cheese in a mixing bowl. Using an electric mixer, beat on medium to high speed until fluffy and light. Add the sour cream, parsley, garlic, oregano, basil, cumin, thyme, lemon juice, salt, and pepper. Mix on low speed until well blended. Makes 11/2 pounds.

For the sandwiches: Slice the baguette in half lengthwise. Place each half cut-side up. Spread 3 tablespoons of the garlic-herb spread on each half. On one half layer the lettuce, tomato, roast beef, and cornichons. Season with salt and pepper. Place the other half of the baguette on top. Slice in half or into smaller pieces.

Makes 2 to 4 servings

Leftover Garlic-Herb Spread is extremely versatile in the kitchen. Use it as a topping for bagels or crackers. It can also be mixed with just-cooked pasta for a simple lunch, or stirred into sautéed spinach for a quick, garlicky creamed spinach.

Griddled Black Forest Ham Sandwiches with Sharp Cheddar Cheese and Cranberry Mustard

These sandwiches are great for those cold and snowy days when you need a little more comfort than just hot soup. Toasted in a pan, they come out warm and crisp, filled with smoky ham and the sharp bite of cheddar cheese. I like to use Black Forest ham, a German variety, because it has a perfect balance of smoky, salty, and sweet flavors. Into the mustard, I mix cranberry sauce to add a tart, colorful New England twist. Dark brown pumpernickel bread matches the German theme of the ham. The sandwich goes really well with Cauliflower, Potato, and Cheese soup (see page 48).

Cranberry mustard

- 1/2 cup homemade honey mustard (see The Drukie on page 208)
- 1/2 cup cranberry sauce

Sandwiches

- 1/3 cup cranberry mustard (from recipe)
- 8 slices pumpernickel bread
- 1 1/2 pounds sliced Black Forest ham
- 8 slices sharp cheddar cheese
- 4 tablespoons butter

▧ For the cranberry mustard: In a small bowl stir together the honey mustard and cranberry sauce until well mixed.

▧ For the sandwiches: Spread the cranberry mustard on each slice of bread. Place the ham on 4 slices of the bread. Place 2 pieces of cheese on top of each slice of ham. Top with the remaining 4 slices of bread. Melt the butter in a large cast iron skillet or heavy sauté pan. Add the sandwiches and pan-fry for 2 minutes on each side. Remove from the pan. Cut each sandwich into four triangles and serve warm.

Makes 4 sandwiches

Lemon and Chive Lobster Rolls

You can't drive far in New England without coming across a sign advertising lobster rolls. They are sold at beachside shacks as well as white tablecloth restaurants. To call this specialty a sandwich gives the wrong impression. It's really a toasted hot dog roll that all but disappears under a mound of chunky lobster salad, made with just a little mayonnaise and seasonings. A leaf or two of lettuce usually lines the bun. This version is easy to prepare at home for your friends as a kickoff to the summer. My sister, Julie, served dozens of these lobster rolls at the anniversary party for her in-laws. They met at Revere Beach, a bustling seaside escape for Bostonians. When they were dating, they often went to Kelly's take-out for lobster rolls with onion rings.

Meat from 4 (1 1/4 pounds each) boiled lobsters, to yield approximately 20 ounces

Juice of 1 lemon

1/4 teaspoon grated lemon zest

2 tablespoons chopped fresh chives

1/3 cup mayonnaise

Kosher salt and freshly ground black pepper, to taste

3 tablespoons butter

4 hot dog buns

■ Chill the lobster meat for at least 1 hour. Cut into large chunks and place in a mixing bowl. Add the lemon juice, lemon zest, chives, mayonnaise, salt, and pepper. Mix gently and set aside.

■ In a heavy sauté pan melt the butter. Place the hot dog buns in the pan and cook until toasted, about 1 1/2 minutes per side. Remove from the pan and place each bun on a plate. Divide the lobster salad into four equal portions and fill each hot dog bun.

Makes 4 servings

For an authentic regional touch, look for "top-loaded" hot dog rolls that are slit on top, instead of on the side. These tend to be softer and less crusty than other hot dog rolls, giving them plenty of surface area for toasting and buttering. For another authentic touch, serve the lobster rolls on rectangular cardboard trays or in baskets just slightly larger than the rolls themselves.

Pulled Chicken with Caraway Coleslaw on Onion Rolls

You can really get down and dirty with this sandwich. It's so very delicious that I never recommend sharing it. Many times I have witnessed a customer hiding in a corner to gobble up this sandwich, hoping not to be recognized while enjoying a messy feast. Big, soft onion rolls hold everything together, but there is always something yummy slipping out. For the maximum amount of crunch and zing, make the coleslaw the same day you assemble the sandwiches.

Caraway Coleslaw

- 2 cups shredded white cabbage
- 1 cup shredded purple cabbage
- 1/2 cup shredded carrots
- 1 scallion, finely, sliced
- 2 heaping tablespoons mayonnaise
- 3 teaspoons whole caraway seeds
- 2 teaspoons apple cider vinegar
- 1 teaspoon sugar
  Kosher salt and freshly ground black pepper, to taste

Sandwiches

- 1 pound cooked chicken pieces
- 4 large fresh onion rolls
- 6 to 8 tablespoons homemade Russian dressing (from Turkey Avocado Club recipe on page 201)
- 4 leaves green leaf lettuce
- 8 slices juicy tomatoes
- 2 cups caraway coleslaw (from recipe)
- 8 crunchy, sweet pickle slices

■ For the caraway coleslaw: Place the white and purple cabbages, carrots, and scallion in a mixing bowl. In a separate bowl whisk together the mayonnaise, caraway seeds, vinegar, sugar, salt, and pepper. Continue whisking until the sugar is dissolved. Pour over the cabbage mixture and toss well.

■ For the sandwiches: Remove the chicken from the bones, discarding the skin and bones. Shred the chicken. Slice each onion roll in half and spread generously with the Russian dressing. On the bottom half of each roll layer 1 lettuce leaf and 2 tomato slices. Pile the pulled chicken on top of the tomatoes. Add a heaping serving of the coleslaw on top of the chicken and top with the pickle slices.

Makes 4 sandwiches

The Drukie

I named this sandwich in honor of my dad, who always has a hankering for Jewish hard salami. If you're patient, you can buy a whole salami and let it harden by hanging it to dry for a couple of weeks. Or walk into a deli and order it at the counter. Whatever method you choose, the salami comes out chewy and garlicky, with just the right amount of flavor and fat to make it irresistible. If you do opt for the deli, ask for some extra slices just for snacking while you prepare the sandwiches. The deli is also a good place to find onion rolls.

Homemade honey mustard offsets the salty salami with a sharp bite. This recipe comes from our family friend, Renee Zalcman. Renee is a great cook who entertains all year, but she is most famous for her Boston Marathon parties, as she lives right beside the annual race route. She is always generous with her recipes, and I am certainly happy that she shared this one with me. It's fun to keep a jar of homemade mustard on hand for a cocktail party, a snack with pretzels, or even a gift. The recipe is easy, and people are impressed when you tell them that you made your own mustard from scratch.

Renee's Homemade Honey Mustard

3/4 cups dry mustard
1 teaspoon black pepper
1 teaspoon cayenne pepper
1 teaspoon white pepper
1/2 cup lukewarm water
1 1/2 cups apple cider vinegar
1 cup honey
2 cups white sugar
1/4 cup packed brown sugar
8 tablespoons butter, melted
3 eggs, lightly beaten

Sandwiches

4 large fresh onion rolls
8 tablespoons homemade honey mustard (from recipe)
1 pound hard salami, sliced
8 slices sharp cheddar cheese
2 cups caraway coleslaw (from Pulled Chicken on page 207)

■ For the homemade honey mustard: In a 4 to 6-quart saucepan add the dry mustard, black, cayenne, and white peppers, and water. Stir until smooth. Add the vinegar, honey, white and brown sugars, butter, and eggs. Bring to a boil over medium-high heat, stirring constantly. Remove from the heat and cool to room temperature. Cover and store in the refrigerator. The mustard will keep at least 1 month in the refrigerator.

Makes 4 cups

■ For the sandwiches: Slice each onion roll in half. Spread each side generously with the honey mustard. Layer slices of hard salami on each side. Add 2 slices of cheddar cheese to each sandwich and top with caraway coleslaw. Place the top half of the roll on each sandwich, insert a toothpick, and slice in half. Serve with kosher dill pickle spears.

Makes 4 sandwiches

Day Boat Sandwiches

photo on
page 194

This sandwich is similar to the famous New Orleans muffaletta. Starting with a large, hollowed loaf of bread, the filling is built from layers of cold cuts, cheese, and vegetables. I then wrap everything tightly so the filling gets compressed and the flavors soak into the bread. Each wedge is packed with colorful ingredients that are substantial enough for a complete meal. I like to make it when Paul and I take a day off to go fishing. We have something delicious to nosh all day while we wait (and wait and wait) for the fish to bite.

1 large round (9 to 10 inches in diameter) crusty bread loaf	6 slices cheese, such as provolone
2 tablespoons chopped fresh basil	1/2 cup roasted red or yellow bell peppers, or a combination
2 tablespoons extra-virgin olive oil	1 jar (4 ounces) marinated artichoke hearts, drained and cut into bite-size pieces
2 cups shredded iceberg lettuce	1/2 cup sliced green olives
2 tomatoes, sliced	1/2 cup sliced black olives
6 ring-shaped slices red onion	1/4 cup pickled hot peppers, cut into rings
1/3 to 1/2 cup vinaigrette or Italian dressing, divided	Kosher salt and freshly ground black pepper, to taste
1/2 pound sliced Genoa salami	
1/2 pound sliced ham, preferably cappicola	

■ With a sharp, serrated knife remove the top 2 inches of the bread. Set the top aside. Using your fingers, hollow out the center of the bread, discarding the bread or reserving for stuffing or croutons.

■ In a small bowl mix together the basil and the olive oil. Using a pastry brush or the back of a spoon, brush the inside of the hollowed-out bread and the inside of the top half of the bread with this mixture. Place the lettuce on the bottom of the hollowed-out loaf. Layer the tomato slices, then the onion slices. Drizzle with 1 to 2 tablespoons of the vinaigrette. Layer the salami, ham, cheese, roasted peppers, artichoke hearts, green and black olives, and hot peppers, drizzling 1 to 2 tablespoons of the vinaigrette between each layer. Season with salt and pepper.

■ Place the top onto the loaf of bread. Wrap the sandwich very tightly with aluminum foil. Let sit at room temperature for at least 1 hour before serving. Cut into wedges or slice into pieces.

Makes 4 sandwiches

This oversized sandwich makes a great alternative to a cold cut tray at a party, especially for a Super Bowl championship. Place the sandwich in the center of a cutting board, slice it into wedges, and let people serve themselves right from the board. For an accompaniment, you can't go wrong with chips and beer, but carrot and celery sticks also give crunchy (and healthy) contrast.

The Fallwich

When our kitchen is filled with the aromas of squash, cranberries, and other seasonal ingredients that we use in our soups, we can't help but raid the pantry for sandwich fillings, too. Why not top freshly roasted turkey with chunks of sweet potatoes? Honey-roasted cashews add crunch and sweetness, and cranberry sauce livens up plain mayonnaise. Everyone likes this sandwich because it's like an entire Thanksgiving dinner between two slices of bread.

Cranberry Mayonnaise

3/4 cup mayonnaise

1/4 cup whole berry cranberry sauce

Sandwiches

2 large sweet potatoes, scrubbed but not peeled

2 tablespoons olive oil

Kosher salt and freshly ground black pepper, to taste

4 individual size (8 inches long each) baguettes

8 tablespoons cranberry mayonnaise (from recipe)

1 1/2 cups baby spinach leaves

1 pound freshly roasted turkey breast, sliced

6 tablespoons honey-roasted cashews

For the cranberry mayonnaise: In a small mixing bowl whisk together the mayonnaise and cranberry sauce until well incorporated.

For the sandwiches: Preheat the oven to 400 degrees. Cut the sweet potatoes into 3-inch chunks. Place in a roasting pan and sprinkle with the olive oil, salt, and pepper. Bake for 30 to 35 minutes, stirring once or twice. Remove from the oven and cool to room temperature.

Slice the baguettes in half lengthwise. Spread each side with the cranberry mayonnaise. Place the spinach leaves on the bottom slice of each baguette. Layer the turkey breast, then the roasted sweet potatoes. Sprinkle with the honey-roasted cashews and season with salt and pepper. Place the top slice of bread on each sandwich.

Makes 4 sandwiches

Salad Days

Salad goes with soup the way ice cream goes with pie. You could eat each type of food separately, but put them together, and you achieve a new level of satiety. At the New England Soup Factory, we always offer a selection of salads. Tuna Niçoise is a summer standard, while potato salad is popular year-round. Other recipes are designed for the limited time when fresh cherries, heirloom tomatoes, or beets are in season. You can have fun mixing and matching each salad with a soup found in an earlier chapter.

I was one of those kids who loved vegetables and salads. A meal never seemed like a real meal unless I had something green and crunchy with it. My favorite combination was fresh, vibrant, crisp vegetables cut into pieces tossed with tangy Wish-Bone Italian dressing and lots of salt and pepper. My dad used to be the official family salad maker until I took his job away. Every night, I made an enormous bowlful that could have easily fed double our family of five. I overestimated on purpose so that I could have seconds, thirds, and maybe even fourths. After dinner each night, my little greasy fingers would still be in the salad bowl, searching for that last radish or cucumber slice. My mother would say, "Marjorie, haven't you had enough? Come on, we're getting ready for dessert." I told my mother I would rather just finish the salad. It drove her crazy that I showed no interest in cake with frosting.

I also liked to pack myself a salad to bring to school. I would save my mom's Cool Whip containers and use them as a bowl. I would find empty pill containers and fill them with the Wishbone dressing. They always leaked, but I didn't care because I had my salad. When I came home from school, I would peel carrots into dozens of thin strips and put them in a big bowl with some kosher salt and Wishbone dressing, of course. I would take my snack into the family room, where I would turn on Julia Child to see what she was making that afternoon—dinner for the boss or pâte à choux or gnocchi and quenelles? Whatever it was, I was spellbound. There were no soap operas or sitcoms for me. I memorized every one of her cooking shows, and I pictured myself making—and devouring—everything.

Israeli Chopped Salad

I have been making this crunchy, refreshing salad since Micki Glucksman moved from Israel to my street in the 1970s. As we were growing up together, I used to love to eat at her house because her mom always made Israeli food, including this salad. It's filled with color and flavor from the bell peppers, tomatoes, scallions, and red onions. The freshly-squeezed lemon juice and fresh mint give it a clean finish. Serve it plain or as a stuffing for pita bread. It also goes well with Homemade Toasted Pita Chips (see Syrian Chickpea Soup recipe on page 106).

2   cucumbers, seeded and diced

2   yellow bell pèppers, seeded and diced small

2   red bell peppers, seeded and diced small

1   red onion, peeled and diced small

1   pound grape tomatoes, cut in half lengthwise

1   bunch scallions, sliced thin

1   can (16 ounces) chickpeas, drained and rinsed

2   tablespoons chopped fresh mint leaves

2   tablespoons chopped fresh flat-leaf parsley

2   cloves garlic, minced

1/2   cup top quality extra-virgin olive oil

2   tablespoons fresh lemon juice

1   tablespoon red wine vinegar
    Kosher salt and freshly ground black pepper, to taste

3   whole wheat pita breads

In a mixing bowl combine the cucumbers, yellow and red peppers, onion, tomatoes, scallions, chickpeas, mint, parsley, and garlic. In a separate small bowl whisk together the olive oil, lemon juice, and vinegar. Drizzle over the vegetables. Season with salt and pepper and toss well. Let sit 30 minutes before serving so the flavors blend.

Pass pita bread at the table for guests to stuff their own sandwiches, or toasted pita chips to serve on the side.

Makes 6 to 8 servings

'Perfect' Potato Salad

I gave this recipe an ambitious name because I've eaten too many potato salads that are far from perfect—ruined by mushy potatoes, goopy dressing, and mayonnaise that dull the flavors. I start this salad with Yukon Gold potatoes, which have a built-in buttery flavor and don't fall apart easily when cooked. Just after they finish cooking, I pour vinaigrette over them so they can absorb the flavor as they cool. The mayonnaise is just enough to hold the salad together. Chopped bell pepper, onion, and pickles add color and crunch. Eggs keep everything fluffy. You can feel proud to bring this salad to any picnic or barbecue.

1   pound Yukon gold potatoes, peeled and cut into bite-size pieces
    Kosher salt, to taste

1/3   cup Red Wine and Herb vinaigrette (see Cobb Salad on page 228) or plain vinaigrette

3/4   cup mayonnaise

2   tablespoons prepared yellow mustard

1 1/2   tablespoons apple cider vinegar

1   tablespoon sugar
    Kosher salt and freshly ground black pepper, to taste

3   tablespoons minced red bell pepper

1/3   cup chopped Vidalia onion

2   dill pickles, chopped

3   hard-boiled eggs

2   tablespoons chopped fresh parsley

Place the potatoes in an 8 to 10-quart pot. Add enough water to cover by 1 inch plus a dash of salt. Bring to a boil over high heat. Reduce the heat to medium and simmer until the potatoes are tender but still hold their shape, about 25 minutes. Drain and place the potatoes in a mixing bowl. Pour the vinaigrette over the potatoes.

In a small mixing bowl stir together the mayonnaise, mustard, vinegar, sugar, salt, and pepper until completely mixed. Set aside.

Add the red pepper, onion, and dill pickles to the potato mixture. Stir gently. Grate the hard-boiled eggs over the top. Add the mayonnaise mixture to the potatoes and stir well. Add the fresh parsley and season with salt and pepper.

Makes 6 to 8 servings

Heirloom Tomato Salad with Crumbled Blue Cheese

Heirloom tomatoes are so special and delicious that it is worth the wait until their arrival at the market in late August. A seller at my local Farmers' Market has won all kinds of awards for her heirloom tomatoes. She describes each one like one of her children. I always visit her booth first because I want to get the first pick. She never lets me in early, even when I am wearing my chef's uniform. The minute the market opens, I rush up and fill my basket. This simple salad dresses the tomatoes up to their best advantage. It would go well with grilled steak, especially rib eye.

5   pounds assorted heirloom tomatoes

1/2 cup sliced Vidalia onion rings

1/4 cup toasted pine nuts

1/2 bunch basil leaves, torn into pieces

1/3 cup crumbled blue cheese

2 1/2 tablespoons balsamic vinegar

5   tablespoons extra-virgin olive oil

     Kosher salt and freshly ground black pepper, to taste

Cut the tomatoes into different shapes, including quarters and slices, and place on a large serving dish. Arrange the onions on top. Sprinkle with the pine nuts, basil, and blue cheese. Drizzle with the vinegar and oil. Generously season with salt and pepper.

Makes 6 to 8 servings

At one time, heirloom tomatoes—tasty, old-fashioned varieties—were almost bred out of existence by large producers who cultivated sturdy (and cardboard-textured) tomatoes that could be shipped without bruising. Thanks to the efforts of dedicated gardeners, heirloom seeds have been preserved and are now widely available. The tomatoes come in odd shapes and sizes, in colors ranging from magenta to zebra-striped. Beautiful they are not, but their flavor is incomparable.

ⓥ Farmers' Market Salad with Chunky Blue Cheese Dressing

photo on page 214

There is nothing quite like the taste of a large, green salad with fresh, locally-grown vegetables. This one takes advantage of tender, buttery lettuce, bracingly crisp cucumbers, and juicy tomatoes that taste like distilled sunshine. There are not many rules when it comes to making this salad, but it is essential to thoroughly wash and dry all of the vegetables to remove dirt and other impurities. You may substitute or add a few of your own selections to the list of vegetables. Make sure to serve the salad well chilled to keep it crisp and refreshing.

Chunky Blue Cheese Dressing

1 1/2 cups mayonnaise

1/3 cup buttermilk

1 cup sour cream

2 tablespoons fresh lemon juice

1 teaspoon Worcestershire sauce

5 dashes Tabasco sauce

1 1/2 cups crumbled blue cheese

Salad

2 heads Boston lettuce, washed and torn into pieces

1 cup chopped purple cabbage

2 pickling cucumbers, peeled and sliced

2 field-grown tomatoes, cut into wedges

5 large red radishes, thinly sliced

1 rib celery, sliced

1 bunch scallions, sliced

1 carrot, peeled and sliced

1 red bell pepper, seeded and sliced into strips

1 yellow bell pepper, seeded and sliced into strips

1 cup yellow cherry tomatoes

Kosher salt and freshly ground black pepper, to taste

1 1/2 cups crunchy croutons (from Vidalia Onion soup recipe on page 12)

Blue cheese dressing (from recipe), to taste

For the blue cheese dressing: In a mixing bowl place the mayonnaise, buttermilk, sour cream, lemon juice, Worcestershire sauce, and Tabasco sauce. Whisk to combine. Add the blue cheese and whisk again until everything is mixed but the blue cheese remains chunky. Refrigerate for at least 1 hour before serving. Makes 1 quart

For the salad: Line a salad bowl with the lettuce leaves. Arrange the cabbage, cucumbers, tomatoes, radishes, celery, scallions, carrot, red and yellow peppers, and yellow tomatoes on top so the different colors are visible. Season with salt and pepper. Sprinkle with the croutons and toss with blue cheese dressing.

Makes 6 servings

Use leftover blue cheese dressing as a dip for raw vegetables, or an accompaniment to spicy Buffalo wings.

Tuna Salade Niçoise with Lemon-Mustard Vinaigrette

You can't go wrong by serving this classic French salad when you are trying to impress someone. It's hearty enough for an entrée, with an array of colorful, filling, and decadent ingredients.

Lemon-Mustard Vinaigrette

- 3/4 cup extra-virgin olive oil
- Juice of 2 large lemons
- 2 tablespoons Dijon mustard
- 2 cloves garlic, minced
- 4 dashes Tabasco sauce
- 1 teaspoon kosher salt
- Freshly ground black pepper, to taste

Salad

- 1 pound fresh green beans, trimmed
- 1 pound red bliss potatoes

- 1 pound mesclun salad greens, washed and dried
- 12 ounces canned tuna, drained
- 2 tablespoons extra-virgin olive oil
- Juice of 1 lemon
- 4 hard-boiled eggs, cut into quarters
- 1 large red tomato, cut into quarters
- 1 cup peeled and diced English cucumbers
- 5 slices red onion
- 1/2 cup niçoise or kalamata olives
- 2 tablespoons capers
- Kosher salt and freshly ground black pepper, to taste

■ For the lemon-mustard vinaigrette: Combine the oil, lemon juice, mustard, garlic, Tabasco sauce, salt, and pepper in a glass jar with a lid. Cover and shake well. Let the flavors blend for at least an hour before serving. Store leftovers in the refrigerator.

■ For the salad: Bring a 4-quart saucepan of salted water to a boil. Add the green beans and

cook for 4 minutes. Remove with a slotted spoon and run under cold water. Set aside to cool.

■ Place the potatoes in a pot of cold water and add a dash of salt. Bring to a boil over high heat. Cook for 5 to 7 minutes. Drain, run under cold water, and set aside to cool. Cut into bite-size pieces.

Line a large serving dish with the mesclun greens. In a small bowl mix the tuna with the olive oil and lemon juice. Place the tuna in the middle of the greens. Around the tuna arrange the eggs, tomato, cucumbers, onion, olives, and capers. Season with salt and pepper. Drizzle with the vinaigrette. Chill in the refrigerator for 30 minutes before serving.

Makes 6 servings

Bing Cherry Chicken Salad with Toasted Pecans

I am partial to chicken salads that contain some fruit. With each bite, you get the savory taste of the chicken with a burst of juicy, cool fruit. Toasted nuts add crunch as well as a savory punch.

Poached Chicken

1¼ pounds skinless, boneless chicken breasts

1 rib celery, cut in half

1/2 onion, peeled

1 slice lemon

1 bay leaf

1 teaspoon kosher salt

Salad

1 cup pecan halves, toasted

Poached chicken (from recipe), cut into bite-size pieces

1/2 cup diced Vidalia onion

1 rib celery, diced small

1/2 pound fresh cherries, pitted

3/4 cup mayonnaise

Kosher salt and freshly ground black pepper, to taste

For the poached chicken: Place the chicken in a 4 to 6-quart pot. Add enough cold water to cover the chicken by 1 inch. Add the celery, onion, lemon slice, bay leaf, and salt. Bring to a boil over medium-high heat. Reduce the heat to medium and simmer for 20 to 25 minutes, or until the chicken is cooked through. Using tongs or a slotted spoon, remove the chicken from the pot. Cool completely and chop before making the salad.

For the salad: Preheat the oven to 350 degrees. Line a baking sheet with foil or parchment paper. Place the pecans in a single layer on the baking sheet. Bake for 5 to 7 minutes, removing once to stir, until fragrant and toasted. Watch carefully to avoid burning.

In a medium mixing bowl place the chicken, onion, celery, cherries, and pecans. Add the mayonnaise and gently stir so that all the contents are lightly covered in mayonnaise. Season with salt and pepper. Refrigerate for at least 1 hour before serving.

Makes 4 to 6 servings

Removing pits from cherries is undeniably tedious, but a cherry pitter (found at most kitchen supply stores) makes the job more tolerable. You'll end up with mushed fruit and stained fingers if you attempt to do it all by hand. For a shortcut, use oven-roasted chicken (even one purchased at the supermarket) instead of poaching the breasts yourself.

California Cobb Salad

Even though most salads are considered light fare, a Cobb salad is substantial enough to make a one-dish meal. Created by Bob Cobb in the 1920s at the Brown Derby restaurant in Los Angeles, it has become a classic that New Englanders enjoy, too. Its combination of salad greens, tomatoes, avocados, chicken, bacon, blue cheese, and hard-boiled eggs supplies you with plenty of vegetables and protein.

Red Wine and Herb Vinaigrette

- 1/3 cup extra-virgin olive oil
- 3 tablespoons red wine vinegar
- 1 clove garlic, minced
- 1/8 teaspoon sugar
- 1/4 teaspoon dried oregano
- 1/4 teaspoon dried basil
- 2 dashes Tabasco sauce
- 1 teaspoon kosher salt
- 1/4 teaspoon freshly ground black pepper

Salad

- 1 head green leaf lettuce, washed and torn into bite-size pieces
- 1 pound cooked boneless chicken breast, diced into bite-sized pieces
- 2 avocados, peeled and diced
- 1 large tomato, diced
- 4 hard-boiled eggs, peeled and chopped into small pieces
- 1/4 cup diced red onion
- 1/2 cup peeled and diced cucumber
- 6 to 8 slices crisp-cooked bacon, crumbled
- 1/2 cup crumbled blue cheese
- 1/2 cup alfalfa sprouts
- 1 tablespoon chopped fresh parsley
  Kosher salt and freshly ground black pepper, to taste
  Red Wine and Herb Vinaigrette, as needed (from recipe)

For the red wine and herb vinaigrette: Place the olive oil, vinegar, garlic, sugar, oregano, basil, Tabasco sauce, salt, and pepper in a glass jar with a lid. Cover and shake well. Shake again right before using. Store leftovers in the refrigerator.

For the salad: Line the bottom of a large (about 12 inches in diameter) serving plate with the lettuce. In the middle, arrange the chicken in a row. Arrange the avocados in a row next to the chicken. Arrange the tomato on the other side of the chicken. Continue to arrange in rows the eggs, onion, cucumber, bacon, blue cheese, and sprouts. Sprinkle the top of the salad with parsley, salt, and pepper. Drizzle with red wine and herb vinaigrette.

Makes 4 to 6 servings

Make your salad more interesting by choosing a specialty bacon, such as smoked applewood. Blue cheese also comes in many varieties, from Italian Gorgonzola to French Roquefort. Ask the manager of the cheese department at your local grocery for a recommendation. Whatever you choose will give your salad a personal finishing touch.

Pan-Roasted Pear and Frisée Salad

The deep, fruity flavor of black fig vinegar is worth seeking out at a gourmet store or from a mail order source. The vinegar is sweetened with black fig juice. My favorite brand is Cuisine Perel fig vinegar. In a pinch, raspberry vinegar may be substituted.

Black Fig Vinaigrette

- 3/4 cup extra-virgin olive oil
- 1/3 cup black Mission fig vinegar or raspberry vinegar
- 2 tablespoons honey
- 2 cloves garlic, minced

  Sea salt and freshly ground black pepper, to taste

Salad

- 2 tablespoons salted butter
- 6 Seckel pears
- 6 cups frisée
- 12 thin slices Vidalia or another sweet onion

  Sea salt and freshly ground black pepper, to taste

  Black fig vinaigrette (from recipe)
- 8 ounces feta cheese, preferably from France

  Seeds from 1 pomegranate

For the black fig vinaigrette: Place the olive oil, vinegar, honey, garlic, salt, and pepper in a bowl or bottle and mix well. Refrigerate leftovers.

For the salad: In a cast-iron skillet or large, heavy sauté pan, melt the butter. Slice each pear in half lengthwise, and remove the seeds with a melon ball scoop. Place the pears, flesh side down, in the pan. Sauté until light brown. Turn over and cook an additional 1 minute. Set aside.

In a large salad bowl or on a platter arrange the frisée and onion slices. Season with salt and pepper. Add 3/4 of the fig vinaigrette. Toss to coat evenly. Place the pear halves on top of the frisée. Crumble the feta on top. Sprinkle the pomegranate seeds on top. Drizzle with the remaining vinaigrette.

Makes 6 to 8 servings

Spinach Salad with Roasted Beets, Green Apples, and Gorgonzola Cheese

 photo on page 233

Beet salads have become popular at Boston restaurants—even among diners who hated eating beets as children. The secret is oven-roasting the beets to bring out their natural, earthy sweetness. An assertive blue cheese or goat cheese stands up well to them. My version of beet salad uses two colors of beets for eye appeal and adds Granny Smith apple slices for a hint of sweetness. Honey-laced dressing made with fruit-flavored vinegar ties everything together.

Fruity Vinaigrette

- 3/4 cup extra-virgin olive oil
- 1/4 cup fig vinegar (see note)
- 1 tablespoon raspberry vinegar
- 2 tablespoons honey
- 2 cloves garlic, minced

  Kosher salt and freshly ground black pepper, to taste

Salad

- 1 bunch (3 or 4) yellow beets, washed and stems trimmed
- 1 bunch (3 or 4) red beets, washed and stems trimmed
- 1 to 2 tablespoons olive oil

  Kosher salt, to taste
- 2 pounds fresh baby spinach

  Freshly ground black pepper, to taste

  Fruity vinaigrette (from recipe)
- 3 Granny Smith apples, sliced
- 1/2 pound Gorgonzola cheese

For the fruity vinaigrette: In a small bowl whisk together the olive oil, fig and raspberry vinegars, honey, garlic, salt, and pepper. Set aside. Whisk again right before using. Refrigerate leftovers.

To make the salad: Preheat the oven to 425 degrees. Place the yellow and red beets on top of two sheets of aluminum foil. Drizzle with the olive oil and sprinkle with salt. Loosely wrap the beets with the foil and scrunch the top to make a package. Place in a roasting pan and bake for 50 minutes. Remove from oven and peel the beets under cold, running water, rubbing the skin off (wear an apron and rubber gloves to avoid stains). Cut the beets into wedges and set aside.

Wash and dry the spinach. Arrange on a large platter. Season with salt and pepper. Drizzle some of the fruity vinaigrette over the spinach and toss gently. Place the apple slices on top of the spinach. Arrange the beets around the salad. Drizzle with more of the fruity vinaigrette over the apples and beets. Crumble the cheese on top and serve immediately.

Makes 6 servings

Raspberry vinegar may be substituted for the fig vinegar. In that case, you'd use 5 tablespoons of raspberry vinegar.

Hearts of Palm Salad with Grilled Shrimp and Avocado

This salad chapter would not be complete without a salad with hearts of palm—one of my favorite foods. Hearts of palm grow mostly in Brazil and Costa Rica, but can also be found in Florida, where they have the far less appealing name of swamp cabbage. Outside of the tropics, they are usually sold in jars or cans. Each pale green stalk is 1/2 to 1 inch in diameter and resembles a cheese stick. They taste like a cross between artichoke hearts and asparagus, with a slightly crunchy, delicate texture. The tropical ingredients in this salad—avocado, macadamia nuts, and lime marinade for the shrimp—complement the hearts of palm well.

1   pound large raw shrimp, peeled and deveined

3   tablespoons olive oil

    Juice of 2 fresh limes

2   cloves garlic, minced

    Kosher salt and freshly ground black pepper, to taste

1   jar (16 ounces) hearts of palm, drained and sliced into 1/2-inch pieces

1   avocado, peeled and sliced

2   tomatoes, cut into wedges

1/4   cup toasted macadamia nuts

1   tablespoon chopped fresh cilantro leaves

1/2   cup lemon mustard vinaigrette (from Tuna Niçoise recipe on page 224)

Place the shrimp in a small ceramic or glass bowl. Add the olive oil, lime juice, garlic, salt, and pepper. Cover and marinate in the refrigerator for 30 minutes. Preheat a grill to medium-high. Place the shrimp on the grill, draining and discarding the marinade. Grill 1 minute on each side, or until the shrimp is perfectly pink and curled up. Remove from the grill and let cool slightly.

Place the shrimp in a mixing bowl. Add the hearts of palm, avocado, tomatoes, macadamia nuts, and cilantro. Gently toss with the vinaigrette. Season with salt and pepper and place in a colorful serving dish. Serve at room temperature.

Makes 4 to 6 servings

Look for hearts of palm packed in jars, because the canned hearts can sometimes be woody and fibrous.

Index

CPSIA information can be obtained
at www.ICGtesting.com
Printed in the USA
LVHW072058061021
699729LV00007B/66

9 780785 256055